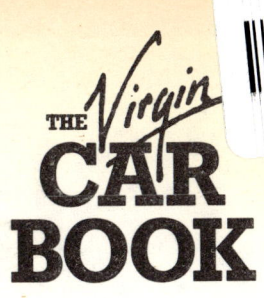

THE Virgin CAR BOOK

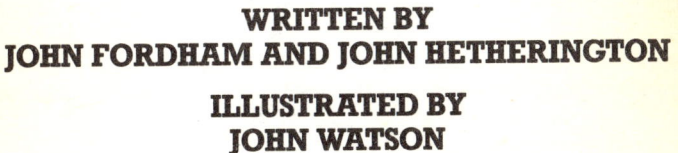

WRITTEN BY
JOHN FORDHAM AND JOHN HETHERINGTON

ILLUSTRATED BY
JOHN WATSON

A Virgin Book
Published in 1988
by the Paperback Division of
W.H. Allen & Co Plc
44 Hill Street
London W1X 8LB

Copyright © 1988 by John Fordham and John Hetherington
Illustrations copyright © 1988 by John Watson

Typeset by Avocet Marketing Services, Bicester, Oxon
Printed and bound in Great Britain by
Cox & Wyman Ltd, Reading

ISBN 0 86369 259 1

CONTENTS

We dedicate this book to our families and friends who have listened to those protestations that we'd 'have it back together again in an hour' with a tolerance beyond the call of love or duty. We would also like to thank those legions of motor car professionals and amateur enthusiasts whose help, advice, good humour and abuse over the years have kept our wheels turning.

1

STATES OF THE ART

'Look here, ignition system, there are these six big holes —
cylinders — in the block and in each one of
them a piston is bobbing up
and down at 50 times a second and what we want you
to do is hit each one of them
on the head with lightning every other time it comes to the top.
Get it? Once you get the rhythm, it'll be a snap.
But you're going to have to be faster than Buddy Rich.'
(John Jerome, Truck, 1977)

At the time of writing, in November 1987, Britain's annual Motorfair was bulging out the walls at London's Earl's Court. Every conceivable kind of road vehicle was represented there. There were the most sophisticated techno-marvels of the state-of-the-art manufacturers, there were modest runabouts, there were stately cars and aggressive cars and cosy cars — and there was the history of the industry in all its spectacular engineering simplicity. Some of those elderly ancestors looked distinctly like mechanical versions of the horse-drawn carriages they were intimately related to.

The occasion was also the opportunity for much press musing. In its motoring special, *The Observer* reported that 1987 was likely to be the year in which more motor cars were sold in Britain than at any other time, and the figure for the year's sales looked as though it would be approaching 1.95 million — 200,000 or so more than three years ago. Fifty-four makes offered hundreds of models at this year's London Motorfair, ranging from the Fiat 126, at £2,430, to the Rolls-Royce Phantom VI, at £207,000 plus. Still within earshot of its 100th birthday celebrations, the motor car continues to go from strength to strength — and though its long-term prospects for doing that don't look so promising, for the time being a car goes on representing a dream of a kind of freedom.

But although the size of the motoring public is expanding all the time, the dimensions of its knowledge of this 20th-century icon are probably diminishing, since an increasing number of vehicles is being sold that are dependent on ever more sophisticated technology. This creates a problem for Joe and Joanna Public, who fear exploitation by knaves and villains in the motor trade, fear holidays, excursions, seductions and trips to the shops in the rain undermined by unexpected mishaps, and fear the devils that can lurk in the machine.

In these pages, we attempt to fill in some of the gaps that make otherwise rational and decisive people helpless defeatists when it comes to the horseless carriage. Some of it is highly technical, and there are technical terms that we can't completely side-step. But acquiring some of this knowledge may save you needless anxieties — and money. After all, if somebody is firmly assuring you that an item of machinery, the name of which you have never heard before and the function of which is an impenetrable mystery to you, is unquestionably in need of expensive replacement, how are you going to know whether to sign on the dotted line or to say you want a second opinion? The only solution, if you're brave enough, is some kind of rudimentary insight into how the whole thing works.

There's no way round it — the names of the bits won't make sense unless you know what their function is, what can go wrong with them and what's involved in putting them right.

MOVERS AND SHAKERS

The motor car truly came into being in 1769, in the form of a steam-powered tricycle built by Joseph Cugnot of Lorraine. But others had toyed with the idea of getting around on wheels without enlisting the help of four-legged friends. Even the mention in Homer's *Iliad* of Vulcan's forays into the motor trade when in one day he constructed 20 tricycles which 'self-moved, obedient to the beck of gods' is judged not to have been the first time anybody thought of the idea.

Later on, Leonardo da Vinci put his mind to it too, and a Swiss clergyman called J. H. Genevois considered the dubious virtues of mounting windmills on a cart, while wind carriages that would travel at 20 mph had been invented in the Netherlands as early as 1600, and some inventors even considered using vast clockwork engines. Air engines — in which the explosion of a gunpowder charge would generate enough air pressure to push a piston down a cylinder — were also entertained for a while, and some as early as the 17th century deployed machinery very close to that subsequently developed for the internal combustion engine — pistons, cylinders and connecting rods, of which more later.

The only version of all this that took root early on was, of course, the steam engine. James Watt's invention, much to his own disgust, was adapted for use in road vehicles from the 1790s, and steam road transport — though always regarded with suspicion by much of the public — long preceded the use of steam on the railways. The horse lobby opposed it, however, the public was scared, and eventually legislation on road speeds became so restrictive that the technology withered away. But the era solved many of the engineering problems that would later be confronted by car designers.

In any piston engine, the fundamental idea is simple. A metal drum is made to be a close fit inside a cylinder. Air or steam under pressure can be forced into the cylinder to push the piston down. A connecting rod and a crank (as in the sketch) converts the up–down motion into a circular motion that can rotate a wheel. On such a simple principle, a vast amount of energy was harnessed and put to use in the Industrial Revolution, and engines for both transportation and industry all made use of it. Between 1862 and 1886 self-powered vehicles were developed by a number of European inventors, all of whom could lay some claim to being the creator of the motor car. Stepping-stones to the final discovery were also laid by a variety of other enthusiasts whose names have now been consigned to the scrap-yards of history.

Consider the problems, as if you were confronted with the unnerving obligation to invent a self-propelled vehicle yourself. Around 1860 or so, the situation would have been as follows:

HOW THE PISTON TURNS THE CRANKSHAFT

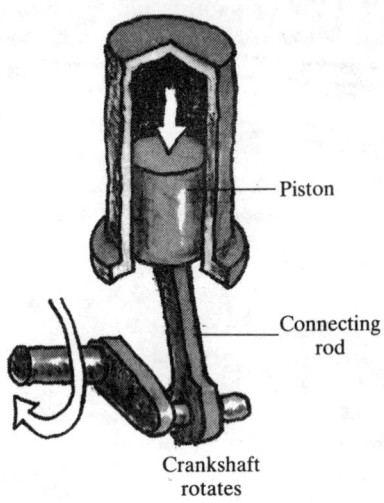

Piston

Connecting
rod

Crankshaft
rotates

★ **Pistons, cylinders and connecting rods** have already been invented, you know how to harness energy in the form of compressed air or steam, and how to turn its up–down action (reciprocating motion) into the rotation of a wheel. So far so good.

★ **Horse-drawn carriages exist**, so a primitive technology has been developed for a passenger-carrying vehicle on four wooden-spoked, metal-rimmed wheels, the worst of the road shocks being borne by cart-springs, or leaf springs. A brake that can apply the simplest kind of friction or obstruction to the rotation of the wheels is also part of the state-of-the-art transportation technology of the day, and oil or acetylene lighting helps travellers to have some idea where they're going in the dark, and pedestrians to have some idea of what they're just about to be hit by.

4

But the problems to be negotiated are formidable. Steam vehicles of the day are heavy and ponderous, require bulky fuel and constant attention while in motion, and need frequent rests to recuperate pressure. Passengers would for the most part be better off walking, not to mention cleaner. The air-powered vehicles of the late 1700s needed back-up almost as complicated — a network of compressor stations supplying air was envisaged at one stage.

Imaginative engineers like yourself are thus preoccupied with the following:

★ **Fuel** — what's needed is something sufficiently volatile to mean that small quantities will liberate enough energy for practical use, without requiring bulky storage on the vehicle. If this can be discovered, then the next snag is finding a means of extracting energy from it.

★ **Ignition** — you have to light the fuel to get the energy out of it to drive your piston. But if the piston is in turn to drive a wheel, and drive it continuously, so that the motion of the car is something better than sporadic, then the strokes of the piston need to be even and regular. The implication of this is that whatever lights the fuel has to do it in a methodical manner. You, or someone you can nick it from, need to come up with a workable ignition system.

But even if you find a satisfactory fuel, and a satisfactory means of systematically setting light to it, that's not the end of the line. Because not only does the ignition have to take place at accurately timed intervals, but also the fuel has to be introduced to the cylinder and the burnt gases removed with the same degree of accuracy if the engine is to run with any kind of rhythm at all. This means that another conundrum you have to put your mind to is:

★ **Breathing** — which means exactly what it says, and pretty much what happens in your lungs. The engine needs to be able to draw in fresh fuel, transform the energy from it and expel the waste without the driver's having to assist the process by hand. One sophisticated mechanical requirement for this operation is that 'doors' to the cylinder open at the right moment to let gas in, close to trap it when the explosion occurs, and open again to let the waste out. Anything that performs such a function is called a valve, and practical valve design is a crucial matter in internal combustion development. Another crucial 'breathing' requirement is that the fuel must enter the engine as a combustible mixture of petrol and air, a phenomenon later to be dubbed 'carburation'.

★ **Cooling** — another snag for the designer. Engines get hot. If something isn't done about this, their moving parts tend to break up or melt, and their casings warp and distort.

All these requirements were a tall order for the budding motor engineers of the late 19th century. Patent rows frequently broke out over who had been the first to devise any of the components of the puzzle. One such, a wrangle over the breathing problem, took place between a German, Nikolaus August Otto, and a Frenchman, Alphonse Beau de Rochas, in the 1870s. These two men devised rival systems for the induction and expulsion of gas. Although Rochas won the patent battle, it was Otto's name that found its way into engineering history. The four-stroke 'Otto cycle', a sequence of piston movements for induction, compression, ignition and exhaust respectively, became the heart of internal combustion technology for a century.

In 1864 Siegfried Marcus, an Austrian engineer, had also run a kind of car. As with many scientific breakthroughs, Marcus's discoveries had at first been accidental. Working on alternative sources of artificial light, he had blithely explored the potential of igniting a petrol and air mixture in a stream of electric sparks. When he recovered from the injuries sustained in this rash experiment, he realized that the reaction of these ingredients was possibly too vigorous for any consumers of domestic illumination not wearing elaborate protective clothing. He had, however, stumbled on electric ignition of petrol or gasoline to produce an impressive bang, and powered a cart with a primitive petrol engine as a result. The breakthrough did not, however, move Marcus to visionary thoughts. He believed the development of the horseless carriage to be 'a senseless waste of time and effort'.

But the fact that the celebration of 100 years of the motor car was based on the vehicles designed by Carl Benz and Gottlieb Daimler in 1885/86 is evidence of how overwhelmingly the credit now lies with these two for taking the whole business more seriously than any of their rivals.

Benz was an obsessive, so much so that many of his contemporaries thought he was suffering from a loose wire. He was, however, convinced that horse-drawn transport would become obsolete in the wake of the motor car. His vehicle was basically a tricycle, with a horseshoe-shaped chassis and a tiller to steer it, like a boat. Though hardly a design of tremendous dash and élan, only three years after the tentative tests of his first model in 1885, Benz had 50 employees building his cars, and the more venturesome members of the public were beginning to catch on.

Running on a parallel track was Gottlieb Daimler, an ex-gunsmith who had been hired by the Otto cycle's disputed originator, Nikolaus Otto, to help him build stationary petrol engines for factories. Otto saw this as his life's work. Although during the 1870's Daimler and Otto substantially developed the technology of the petrol engine, the former had dreams about road transport that the latter did not. Daimler eventually left the firm to explore his own design for a single-cylinder air-cooled petrol engine that could power a car. He achieved it in the same year that the Benz tricycle appeared, and then pursued a policy of converting horse-drawn carriages to petrol engines.

Between the mid-1880s and the end of the century, the motor industry took off, and some of its most famous names — De Dion Bouton, Panhard-Levassor, Packard, Olds, Ford — opened for business. And it was Henry Ford, convinced that the motor car could be everyday transport rather than simply a toy for the wealthy, who set in motion a revolution. Technical developments helped it on its way. The electric self-starter, for instance, did away with the backbreaking exertions of swinging a crank handle to start the car and expanded the potential market beyond the ranks of the muscular or those who could afford chauffeurs with powerful biceps. By 1920, much of the United States' economy was already underpinned by automobile production, and the names of Austin and Morris in Britain, Fiat in Italy and Citroën in France became household words. The world was getting used to being on motorised wheels.

The explorations of the 19th-century pioneers were made more robust, reliable and flexible during the years of the motor car's rise to fame, but they remained similar in principle to the original doodlings on the drawing-boards in obscure workshops throughout Europe. In any conventional motor car today, the principles — though extensively adapted and developed — are virtually unaltered. A little motoring history may have given you a glimmer of the fundamental problems requiring to be solved. A rundown of the anatomy of the motor car today may reveal the layers of sophisticated development that have enveloped them.

2

UNDER THE SKIN

'Just by looking at the machine, I . . . grasped all the intricacies of the mechanism.'
(Ettore Bugatti, describing his first meeting with the De Dion Bouton)

'I may say my car is a perfect dream. It is so reliable I have done away with my carriages and horses.'
(Rolls-Royce customer, The Autocar, 1907)

A modern motor car, although it comes in all shapes and sizes, is fundamentally a metal box on four wheels. In Benz's day it wasn't a box at all, but more or less a bench seat on a metal frame from which the working parts were suspended. Until the 1950s, though, it often looked like a box. It was actually a collection of metal panels fastened on a chassis — a rugged metal frame that carried the machinery. But by the 1950s, with the development (through rapid strides in the machine-tool industry) of the monocoque or rigid-box metal body, the separate chassis had become a thing of the past. Although Citroën had made use of this development for their revolutionary Tractions since the mid-thirties, it had otherwise been slow to displace the old habits of the coach-building trade.

The monocoque had virtues and drawbacks. It lightened the car, and thus meant that more of that expensive power could be used to propel the vehicle rather than get absorbed in the machine's own dead weight. It made cars roomier inside, simpler and cheaper to produce, and less prone to leaks, creaks, attacks on the woodwork by the elements and so on. But it also meant that a car's bodywork was now integral to its structural soundness. Serious corrosion in the sections contributing most to its rigidity and stability — the 'box sections' under the doors, the mounting points of the suspension and the steering — could make the vehicle a virtual write-off.

THE MACHINERY

The mechanics of a motor car involve the collusion of a variety of subsystems, all of them contributing to the objective of moving the human race through the scenery with the minimum inconvenience. As we've already considered, the heart of an engine is a reciprocating piston which has to be 'serviced' by a valve system to let gas in and waste out, an ignition system to ignite it, a fuel system to supply petrol and to mix it with appropriate quantities of air, and cooling and lubrication systems to stop all the thrashing bits of hot metalwork from melting. Here's a thumbnail sketch of those systems, including some of the terminology associated with them that you might find propelled towards you in the service department of your friendly local garage:

THE ENGINE

This is still usually mounted in the front of the car, although a few vehicles opt for rear mounting, as the Volkswagen Beetle did for four decades. Nowadays the number of cylinders used on production cars is most frequently four, although some more powerful vehicles have six or eight, which boosts smoothness and performance — and fuel bills. Cylinders are generally arranged in a line, although on some engines they are grouped in opposing banks in a V-shaped arrangement (the meaning of expressions like 'V6' and 'V8' as applied to motor cars) or even horizontally, another feature of the rear-engined VW. The sketch shows the engine's fundamental moving parts, which are:

SINGLE-CYLINDER EXAMPLE

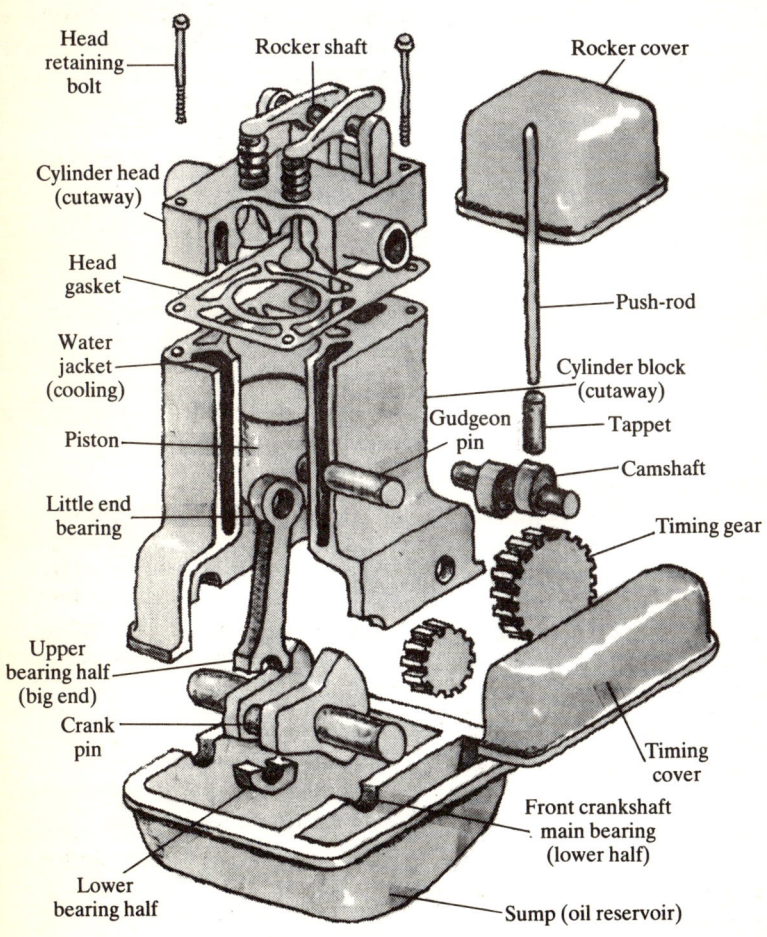

Head retaining bolt

Rocker shaft

Rocker cover

Cylinder head (cutaway)

Head gasket

Water jacket (cooling)

Push-rod

Cylinder block (cutaway)

Piston

Gudgeon pin

Tappet

Camshaft

Little end bearing

Timing gear

Upper bearing half (big end)

Crank pin

Timing cover

Front crankshaft main bearing (lower half)

Lower bearing half

Sump (oil reservoir)

- **The cylinder block** — a casting of iron or aluminium bored out to house the pistons and the shaft (crankshaft) rotated by their reciprocating action.

- **The pistons and connecting rods** — usually alloy castings, fitted with sprung rings to maximize their gas-tightness, connected to the crankshaft by steel rods.

- **The crankshaft** — a steel forging, very strong, and constructed with the connecting points (bearings) for the rods being offset so that the up–down movement of the rods can rotate it, much as the reciprocating action of your descending foot is converted into rotation by the offset position of a bicycle pedal in relation to the centre of the chainwheel. A crankshaft for a four-cylinder engine will be arranged such that two of the four pistons will be at the top of their stroke while the other two are at the bottom.

If you've grasped that much, then it might now be possible to get the hang of the Otto cycle we mentioned earlier, as applied to a modern four-cylinder car. The Otto cycle works in these stages:

- **Induction** —fuel is drawn into the cylinder through a valve by the suction of the piston descending the cylinder.

- **Compression** — as the piston rises again it compresses the gas into a small space to maximize the potential of energy unleashed. This ascending stroke coincides with the closing of valves into the cylinder so that the space is completely gas-tight.

- **Power** — at this point in the cycle a carefully timed electric spark ignites the gas. The piston is driven forcibly to the bottom of the bore by the explosion, pulling the crankshaft round to bring the other pair of pistons to the top of the bores, and in the process rotating the transmission of the car. This is the way power is applied to the roadwheels.

- **Exhaust** — when our piston completes its downward journey, it is forced to rise again by an explosion in another cylinder and another part of the sequence. This ascending stroke coincides with the opening of a second valve in the cylinder, and the rising piston squeezes the burnt gas through it and out into the car's exhaust.

However much or little you understand about things mechanical, it might be apparent from the above that the conversion of petrol into

THE FOUR-STROKE CYCLE

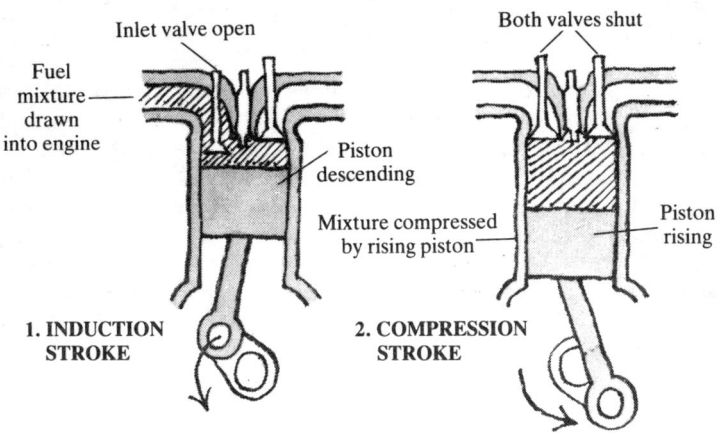

Inlet valve open

Fuel
mixture
drawn
into engine

Piston
descending

**1. INDUCTION
STROKE**

Both valves shut

Mixture compressed
by rising piston

Piston
rising

**2. COMPRESSION
STROKE**

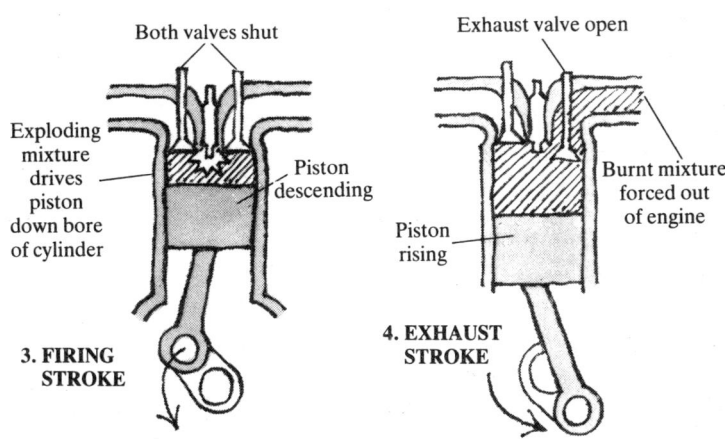

Both valves shut

Exploding
mixture
drives
piston
down bore
of cylinder

Piston
descending

**3. FIRING
STROKE**

Exhaust valve open

Burnt mixture
forced out
of engine

Piston
rising

**4. EXHAUST
STROKE**

movement which eventually arrives at your car's wheels — or, to put it more scientifically, the release of heat from the fuel which expands in a confined space to propel a piston or pistons — is a relatively simple process. But proper running of the engine is a complex matter involving precise timing, specific quantities of fuel, and accurate machining of components to arrive at gas-tight fits where it counts.

When you hear the language of 'tuning up' motor cars, it tends to be the supply of just the right quantity of petrol and the timing and strength of the electric spark that are being adjusted. More major surgery is required when parts of the actual carcass of the engine are wearing out. For instance, the valves that let the gas in and out of the cylinders are no longer a good enough fit for the mixture to be compressed without leaking, or the pistons themselves have become a sloppy fit in their bores, with the same result. All such ailments are noticeable to the driver in the form of the car's becoming asthmatic on hills, noisy, hard to start, or invisible beneath a cloud of blue smoke.

ANCILLARIES

Another mysterious mechanical notion you might have heard of in the context of engines is the **flywheel**. A flywheel is simply a wheel that is heavy enough, when set spinning, to carry on spinning under the force of its own weight for some time. You might imagine that if power is already being produced by combustion you don't need anything else to help the crankshaft go round, but the flywheel is there to smooth out the jerkiness caused by the succession of explosions in the cylinders.

The simpler the engine, the more the flywheel has to do. In a single-cylinder engine, for instance, a heavy flywheel is required to bring the piston back through its ascending stroke after the explosion has driven it down. Where there are several cylinders, as in most cars, a sequence of firing strokes does much of this work, which means that a much lighter flywheel can be used.

In the drawing on page 11 you can see a simplified version of the carcass of an average motor-car engine. The pistons, their connecting rods and the crankshaft are usually housed in a single iron or aluminium casting called the **crankcase**. The pistons, generally aluminium for lightness and coolness, have several sprung rings around their circumference to make the piston as gas-tight as possible in the cylinder. These **piston rings** not only keep the gas in the space above the piston and under sufficient compression to ignite effectively, but also prevent the oil lubricating the cylinders from mixing with the burning fuel and producing plumes of blue smoke at the exhaust.

The **connecting rods** are usually made of steel and take a fearful battering in the 100-times-a-second up – down movement they may go through when the engine is running fast. The **bearings** which link connecting rods to the other components are similarly bludgeoned. A small bearing called the **little end** lives inside the piston itself, and a much larger one, the **big end**, at the crankshaft end. The big ends particularly need to be copiously, cleanly and reliably lubricated if they aren't to wear quickly.

With this in mind, engineers have tended to ensure that the rubbing surfaces on the connecting rod big end are made of an oil-retaining solder-like metal, and the corresponding surface on the crankshaft of hardened and polished steel. A similar arrangement is used for the large and crucial bearings in which the crankshaft runs in the crankcase. Bearing failure is usually an indication of an engine that has run a high mileage, or has been run for a long time on dirty oil. Modern lubricants and manufacturing materials have made it a far less common form of breakdown than it used to be on early cars, when no journey was fun unless it involved a couple of engine rebuilds *en route*.

Also generally housed in the crankcase is a **camshaft** or camshafts, linked to the rotation of the crank by a device very similar to a bicycle chain, although gears or belts can be used instead. The camshaft is a steel rod with bumps or protrusions strategically arranged around the surface along its length. As it rotates, these bumps (or **cams**) can push a series of rods (**tappets**, connected to **push-rods**) up and down in a predetermined sequence, to open and close the valves at the right times to get the gas in and out of each cylinder. The valves are simply discs about the size of a 10p piece, with a stem running from their centres which is periodically pushed open by the action of the cams and push-rods, and closes again through the action of strong springs surrounding each valve.

All these bits and pieces are usually housed in another heavy chunk of metal that is bolted tightly on top of the crankcase. This chunk is called the **cylinder head**, and is detachable so that the valve gear can be serviced without the need to remove the entire engine. The valve gear consists of the valves themselves, their springs, and a number of see-sawing pivoted metal arms (**rockers**) — corresponding to the number of valves there are — which bear on the ends of the valve stems.

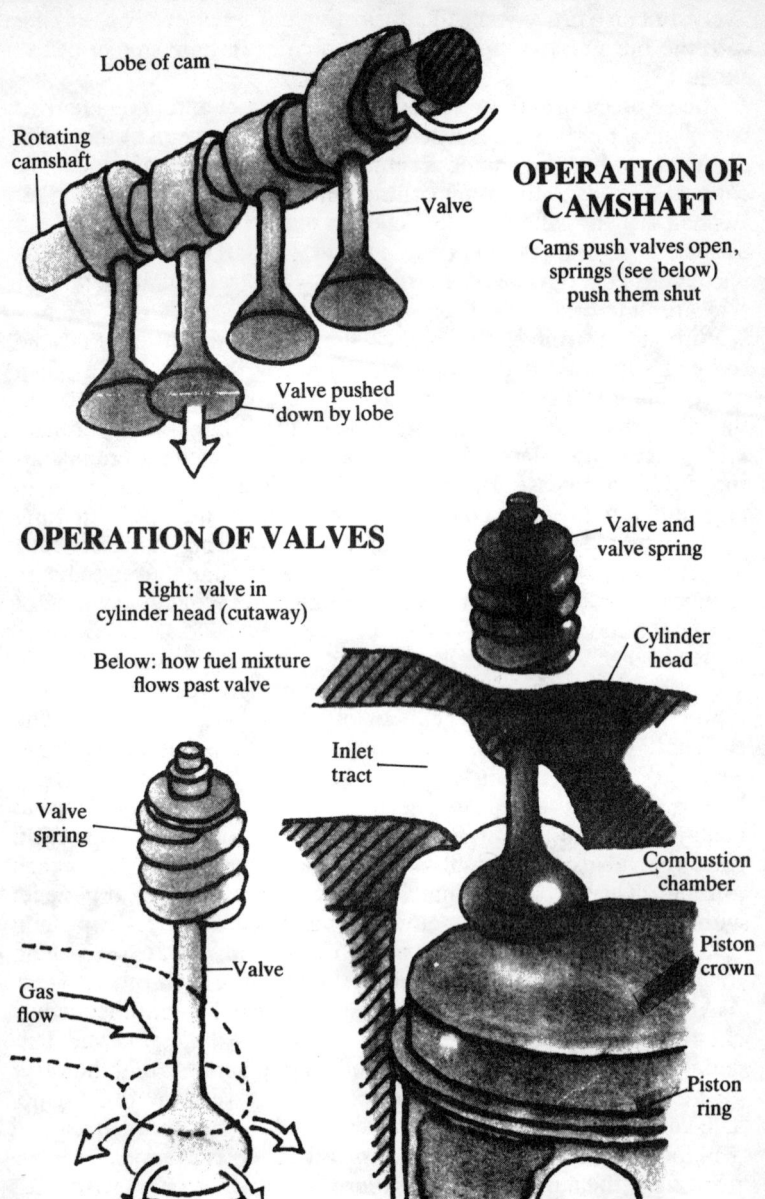

Lobe of cam

Rotating camshaft

Valve

Valve pushed down by lobe

OPERATION OF CAMSHAFT

Cams push valves open, springs (see below) push them shut

OPERATION OF VALVES

Right: valve in cylinder head (cutaway)

Below: how fuel mixture flows past valve

Valve and valve spring

Cylinder head

Inlet tract

Combustion chamber

Piston crown

Piston ring

Valve spring

Gas flow

Valve

As you can deduce from the drawing, since the valves have to be leant on from *above* in order to open over the pistons, and the rotating camshaft is usually *lower* than them in the engine because its home is the crankcase, something has to turn the upward movement of the push-rods (which are forced upwards by the bumps on the camshaft) into a *downward* movement to open the valves. This is the work of the rockers. The rising push-rod tips up one end of the see-saw and the other end tips down on to the valve stem, forcing it open.

We've used the expression 'generally' or 'usually' because not all engines are built alike. Some high-performance cars have done away with the complications and energy-absorption of push-rods and tappets, and have a cam or a pair of cams mounted *above* the cylinder head, bearing directly on the valves. This can be an arrangement that is harder to make adjustments to, but it complies with some fundamental engineering recommendations for having the minimum of moving parts that can swallow so much of the precious and expensive energy being generated by the engine.

Many things that are bolted to one another in engines require **gaskets** or seals to be sandwiched between the metal parts to prevent leaks of fluids or gases. Between the cylinder head and the crankcase, there is the biggest seal of all — a compressible copper-and-fibre sheet, with holes cut in it for the cylinders, push-rods and cooling waterways, called the **head gasket**. Leakages are rare but may happen if some other fault causes the engine to overheat and the metal parts to distort. The result is that the performance of the engine will be noticeably affected.

TIMING

As we've seen, there's no room for late arrivals in the internal combustion cycle. Valves have to open and close, sparks have to spark, and pistons have to ascend and descend at just the right moments or there is no hope of the engine developing its proper power. The pistons and the crankshaft, the treadmill of the operation, just go on up and down, round and round, until the cows come home. The brain behind the co-ordination of all the services that keeps this relentless movement going is the **camshaft**, and some engine designs have one camshaft for the inlet valves and a second one for the exhausts.

As we've described the crank is linked to the camshaft. The arrangement of the gearing determines that for every turn the crankshaft makes, the camshaft makes a half-revolution, because, as you can see, if you look at the drawing on page 13, the Otto cycle of induction/compression/expansion and exhaust takes two full turns of the crankshaft to achieve, not just one.

Valve operation — the camshaft arranges that when the piston is descending on the **induction** stroke (drawing in petrol vapour), the **inlet valve** to that cylinder is open. When the piston reaches the bottom of the cylinder and starts to rise again, the inlet valve closes, and the gas is compressed until it takes up only the space available in the cylinder head above the top of the fully-risen piston (the **combustion chamber**). Ignition and expansion then take place, the piston is driven to the bottom of the bore, and as it rises again, the **exhaust valve** is opened by the revolving camshaft and the spent gas expelled. In practice there is some overlap between the openings and the closings of the inlet and exhaust valves to improve the flow of gas, but this is not of immense interest unless you're planning on taking this book as the starting point of a career in engine design.

IGNITION

If the gas has to enter the combustion chamber at a precisely-timed moment, the spark that ignites it has to be similarly co-ordinated. Not only that, but to make things trickier, it has long been recognized that the timing of the spark should vary according to different driving conditions — going uphill or under heavy load as opposed to going fast on a level road with the accelerator only partly depressed, for instance. In general, the faster the engine is running, the longer the period (even though it is only a fraction of a second) the fuel needs to burn, and therefore the earlier the spark needs to be.

So a system has to exist that can:

- **Generate** a series of high-voltage sparks from the low-voltage battery that is as much of an electrical power source as a car is capable of carrying.

- **Distribute** these sparks to each of the engine's cylinders in turn, and at precisely the right moment in the cycle of each cylinder.

- **Adjust** the timing of the spark according to the prevailing driving conditions.

The system that achieves all these miracles is called the **ignition system**. Until recently it was always a mechanical arrangement in which things revolved and opened and closed, and centrifugal weights flapped about. Latterly, microtechnology has made **elec-tronic** ignitions popular because the elimination of many moving parts has intervened in one of the areas most frequently responsible for everyday breakdowns. But mechanical systems are still the arrangements in common use today.

Starting at the end we're already familiar with, the hot-spot above the piston where combustion takes place, this is where the spark that is generated ends up — or it does if everything's working as it should be. Screwed into the combustion chamber space above the piston is a **sparking plug** — one to each cylinder. The sparking plug is simply an electrode that receives the high-voltage pulse from the ignition system.

To understand how this works, we have to take a step back and fill in a detail about a motor car's electrical system. Since the vehicle's not much use to anybody if it has always to remain within easy reach of a mains plug, it has to have a self-contained electrical source — a battery. And, as you'll know if you've ever wired a plug, electricity has to flow on a **circuit** — out from the power source to the appliance, and back again to the power source. To minimize the amount of wiring the car needs, cables run from only one side of the battery to the electrical devices. The 'return' or **earth** is achieved through the car's bodywork itself, and since a car's electrics work only on a harmless 12-volt system, you never notice this if you touch the metalwork.

This helps us to understand our **sparking plug**. The electrical pulse is fed into the sharp end, as it were, and travels down an electrode in the centre of the plug, which is insulated from the engine and the rest of the bodywork by high-resistance ceramic material. The only way the impulse can complete its natural journey by 'escaping to earth' is by jumping across a gap between the central electrode and the threaded part of the plug, which is the bit that connects to earth via the metalwork of the engine. As it does this, a spark — the fatter and bluer the better — is created in the combustion chamber, just at the instant when the gas is in a nicely volatile and highly compressed state. Since we've described the Otto cycle in some detail, you know the rest.

The search for the source of the spark — from the point of view of explaining the ignition system, we have of course considered the effect before the cause. How does a high-voltage pulse of electricity arrive at the plug in the first place, since the only voltage source on the car is a *low*-voltage one? How does it arrive at all the engine's cylinders in the correct sequence and at the right time? And even more niftily, how does the timing of the spark vary according to the driving conditions as we described earlier?

Let's take these hard questions in order:

★ **Spark generation**. The high-voltage pulse is created because physicists a long time ago discovered something useful about electricity, to whit: if you run a current into a coil of thin wire, with a coil of thick wire next to it, and both are wound around a magnet, then a sharp interruption of that current will 'step up' the voltage massively, though only for an instant. The gadget that does this is called an **induction coil**, but will be described simply as 'the coil' by mechanics.

The device that effects the necessary interruption of the current is called the **contact-breaker**, which once again will usually be termed 'the points' in the workshop. This is simply a tiny switch, flicked open and shut by a rotating cam, geared to our 'managerial' component, the camshaft. The bits and pieces are set up so that the opening and closing of the points coincides with the firing position of the piston and the valves in each cylinder.

You should now be able to follow in the sketch the electrical path that produces the spark. A wire supplies current to the **primary** winding of the coil, but it can complete the circuit to earth only via the **points**, which allow it to do so when they're closed, but not when they're open. At each interruption, a high-voltage pulse emerges from the **secondary** coil. This is the spark the engine needs to run. You can also see in the drawing a further subcircuit in the path to earth, which is represented by that symbol like an inverted Christmas tree. This is the **condenser**, another small device sometimes causing running problems out of all proportion to its modest dimensions. Without going into unnecessary detail, the condenser's job is to 'buffer' the spark, and reduce its tendency to burn the contact-breaker points.

★ **Distribution**. The question now is how to get the spark to all the cylinders in the right order. Not surprisingly, the gadget that achieves this is called the **distributor**, another term that almost everyone has heard of in association with cars, but possibly with total mystification.

In practice, the contact-breaker points and the distribution arrangements are generally housed in the same unit these days, and

IGNITION SYSTEM CIRCUIT DIAGRAM

Primary circuit runs from coil to moving contact mechanism. Fixed contact runs to earth. When points are closed, primary circuit is complete and runs to earth.

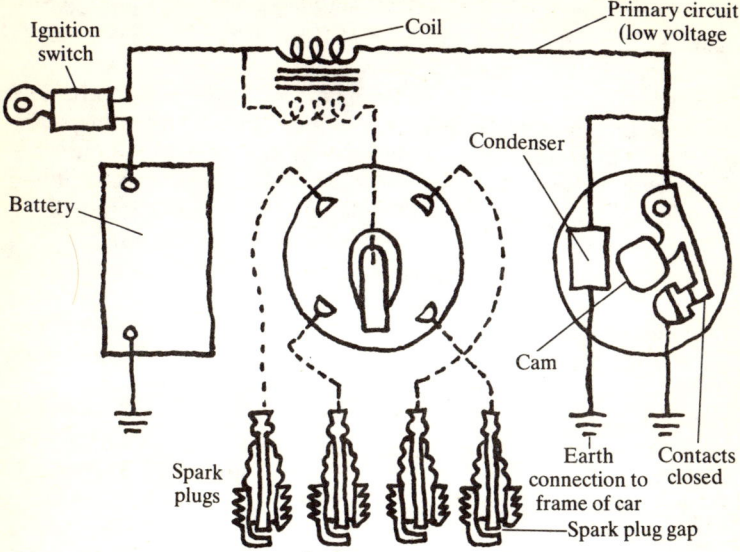

When contacts are opened (by cam) primary circuit is broken. High voltage is induced at coil in secondary circuit, and passes via rotating rotor arm to spark plug and finally to earth after jumping plug gap.

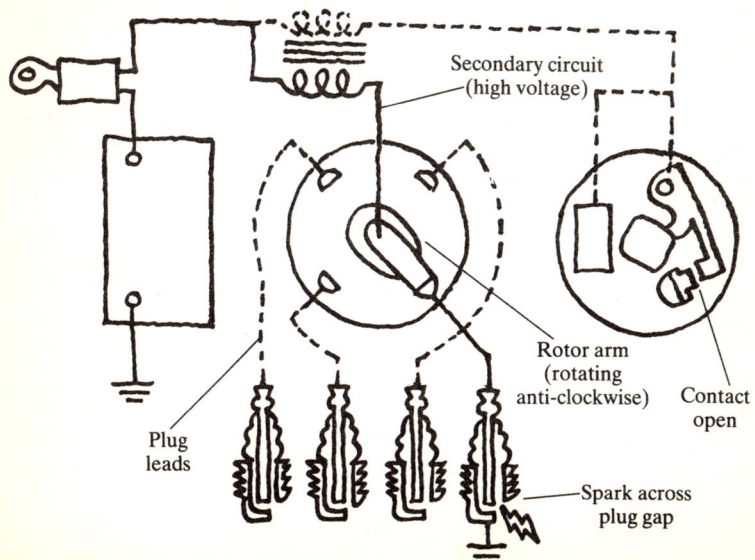

the term 'distributor' covers both functions (see sketch). A spindle down the centre of it is geared to the famous camshaft. The upper section of the spindle is shaped in the form of four (or six, or eight, or however many cylinders the engine has) small **cams** bearing against the contact-breaker. All this means is that there is a section of the spindle where it's effectively square instead of round.

As the spindle rotates when the engine is running, the 'corners' of the spindle (in other words, the cams) push open the contact-breaker, which closes again under its own spring action as the 'flats' of the cams pass by. All this, needless to say, is happening ludicrously fast, and you wouldn't be able to witness the action with the naked eye — which is why, as we'll see later, careful maintenance of the distributor parts is essential to reliable running, and a source of many problems when neglected.

So much for the contact-breaker. Above it within the distributor unit there is also a spinning **rotor**, like a propeller with only a single blade. The blade is brass, embedded in the moulded body of the rotor. The body is made of a non-conducting material so that a spark supplied to the blade goes where it's intended to, rather than bunking off down the spindle of the distributor instead. The rotor is what distributes the spark to the cylinders.

Clipped on to the top of the distributor is a thick cup-like device (the **distributor cap**), which is also made of a moulded non-conductive material, with a ring of brass contacts (one for each cylinder) bonded into it, and a central contact to receive the spark-supplying cable from the coil. The central contact turns into a sprung carbon rod, looking a bit like a piece of graphite from a very fat lead pencil, and this is pressed by a small spring against the centre of the spinning rotor. The rotor whirls round, supplied with a stream of sparks from the coil, which then pass in the proper order to each of the ring of brass contacts surrounding it in the distributor cap. Heavy insulated cables from each of the contacts pass out of the distributor cap to their appropriate sparking plugs.

★ **Ignition timing**. But if this is how the basics of ignition are established, how about the subtleties like varying the timing of the spark according to whether you're driving up a hill with an elephant on the roofrack or cruising along a motorway as free as a bird? There are a couple of further variations, and then we're out of this treacherous territory. If the timing were to occur only at one unchangeable moment, then we could just bolt the distributor to the side of the engine, with its spindle linked to the cam, and leave

DISTRIBUTOR COMPONENTS

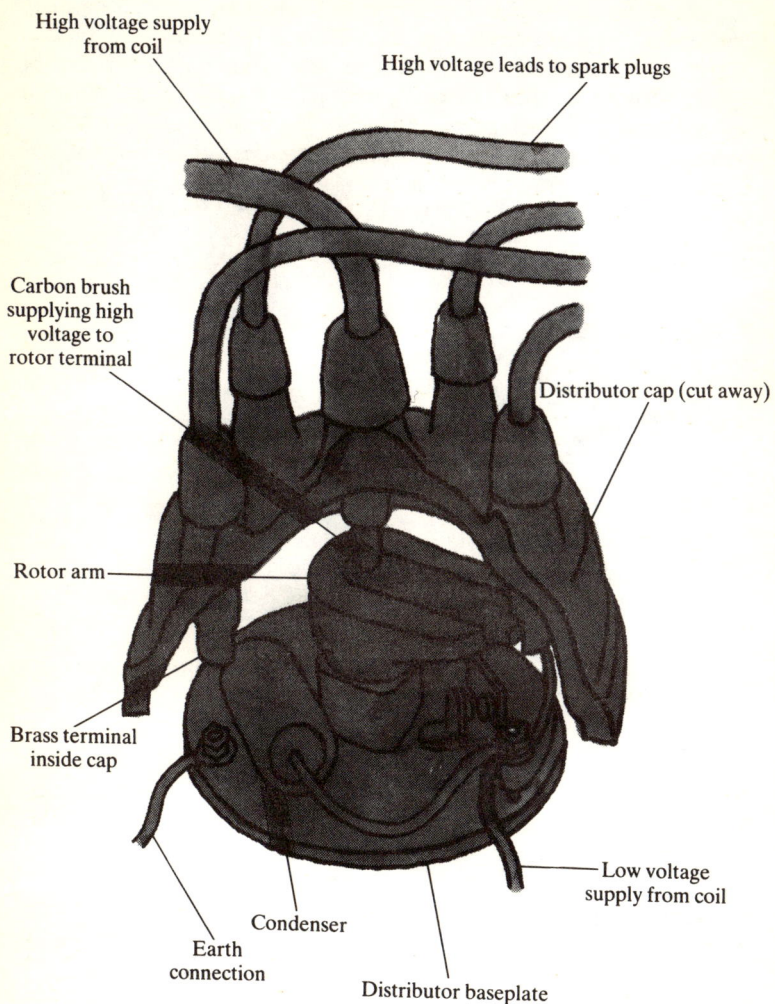

High voltage supply from coil

High voltage leads to spark plugs

Carbon brush supplying high voltage to rotor terminal

Distributor cap (cut away)

Rotor arm

Brass terminal inside cap

Low voltage supply from coil

Earth connection

Condenser

Distributor baseplate

it at that. In fact, the distributor is bolted to the engine in such a way that the entire body of the unit can rotate *around* the spindle. If you think about it, this means that the spindle and its 'square' section or cams can go on spinning in only one position, but the contact-breaker it bears on can change its position in relation to the spindle. If you turn the distributor body one way, you can thus make the spark happen 'earlier' (because the cam is hitting the breaker sooner than it did) or 'later'.

The engineering terminology for this is, once again, fairly logical

MECHANICAL ADVANCE MECHANISM

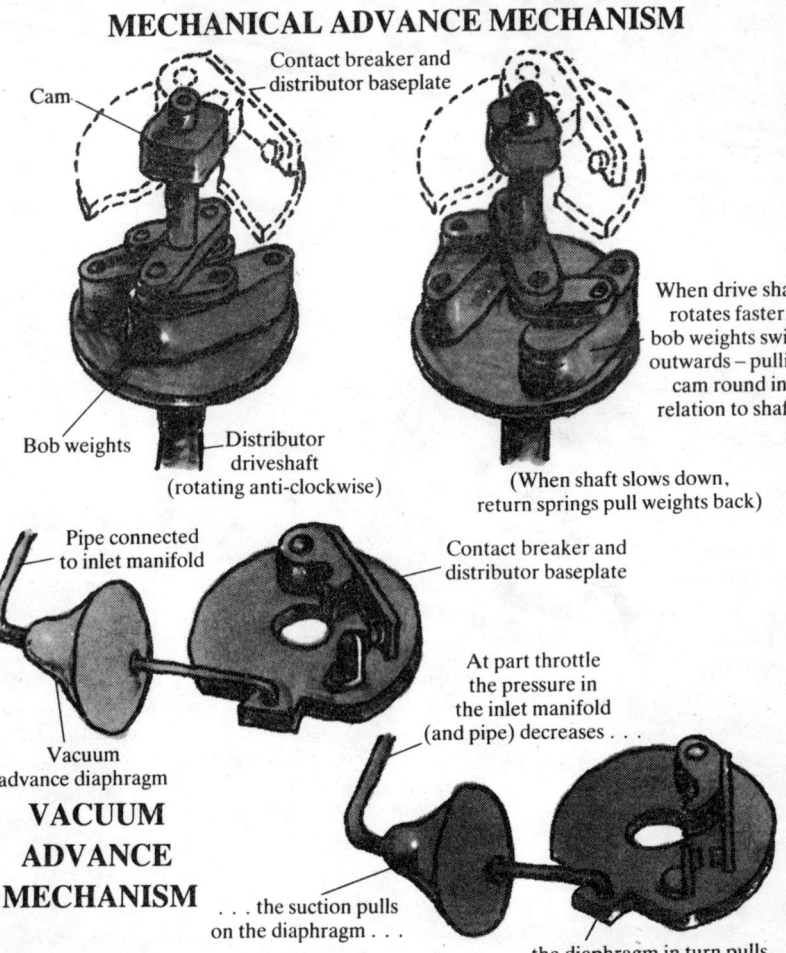

Contact breaker and distributor baseplate

Cam

When drive shaft rotates faster, bob weights swing outwards – pulling cam round in relation to shaft.

Bob weights

Distributor driveshaft (rotating anti-clockwise)

(When shaft slows down, return springs pull weights back)

Pipe connected to inlet manifold

Contact breaker and distributor baseplate

At part throttle the pressure in the inlet manifold (and pipe) decreases . . .

Vacuum advance diaphragm

VACUUM ADVANCE MECHANISM

. . . the suction pulls on the diaphragm . . .

. . . the diaphragm in turn pulls the contact breaker around in relation to the cam, so 'advancing' the spark

— it's called 'advancing' or 'retarding' the spark. Ideally, the engine needs the spark to happen sooner the faster it's running, to allow an extra fraction of a second for the fuel to burn in. It also needs to be advanced when the engine is under light load and the accelerator only partly depressed, because when the engine's compressions are lower, the fuel burns more slowly.

Modern vehicles achieve these effects in two ways. Below the contact-breaker unit, two centrifugal weights — which move *away* from the spindle when the engine is running fast, and *closer* to it when the rotation is slower — are linked to the contact-breaker and slightly alter its position according to engine speed. A vacuum device linked by a tube to the engine's gas intake also 'senses' whether the accelerator is fully or partly depressed, and similarly pulls and pushes the baseplate on which the contact-breaker is mounted. Failures of these devices won't stop the car, but they will certainly impair its running and if left to themselves may eventually cause an engine failure, of which more later.

Now we know how the engine is built, and how the spark is co-ordinated with the movements of the pistons and valves. But so far, we have simply considered that some mysterious entity called 'the gas' gets pumped into the combustion chambers out of nowhere. After all, you don't replenish gas cylinders in your motor car, you go to a petrol station, pour a lot of smelly expensive liquid into it, and occasionally win sets of naff teacups for your trouble. What happens to this stuff after you pour it into that ever-unsatisfied black hole at the back of your pride and joy?

Petrol is stored in a metal tank, usually under the back seat, or at the front of a rear-engined car — either way, as far away from the heat and sparks as possible. A tube from this tank runs to a **fuel-pump**, which may be near the tank or in the engine compartment. Some pumps are electrically operated, some run off the ubiquitous camshaft. In the electric ones, a kind of electric motor that produces sliding horizontal movement rather than rotational movement (a **solenoid**) pushes forward a fibre diaphragm, which has an effect pretty much like that of the diaphragm inside your chest. The movement creates a vacuum, which is filled by whatever the space behind the diaphragm is linked to — air in the case of your chest, petrol in the case of the fuel pump. The vacuum sucks the fuel from the tank to the pump, a valve closes to stop it going back where it came from, and the reciprocating action of the diaphragm forces the fuel up to the gadget that transfers it to the eagerly awaiting combustion chambers.

MECHANICAL FUEL PUMPS

When the diaphragm moves downwards, fuel is drawn into the pump through a non-return valve. When the diaphragm moves upwards, fuel is forced out of the pump through another valve.

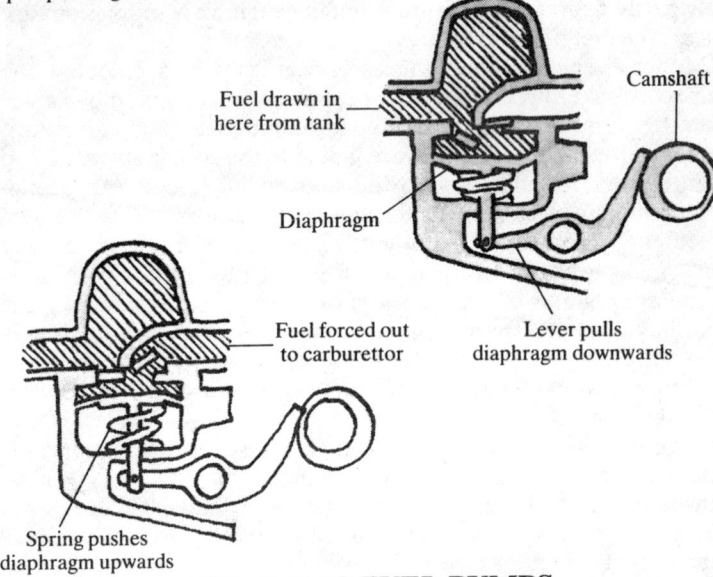

Fuel drawn in here from tank

Camshaft

Diaphragm

Fuel forced out to carburettor

Lever pulls diaphragm downwards

Spring pushes diaphragm upwards

ELECTRIC FUEL PUMPS

Electric pumps work on similar principle, except that action of diaphragm is controlled by an electromagnet instead of the cam.

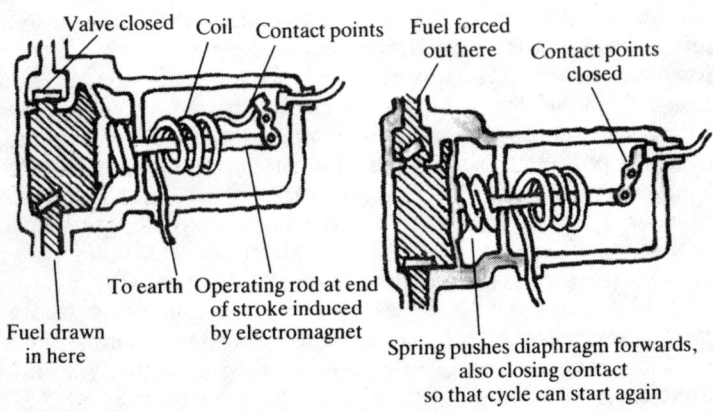

Valve closed   Coil   Contact points   Fuel forced out here   Contact points closed

To earth   Operating rod at end of stroke induced by electromagnet

Fuel drawn in here

Spring pushes diaphragm forwards, also closing contact so that cycle can start again

26

CARBURATION

Like the distributor, most people have heard of the **carburettor** without assuming it's a pasta dish or the name of an opera. They may also have a vague idea that it's something to do with the car's fuel system without knowing quite what it's intended to achieve and why.

Carburettors can be fiendishly complicated things in practice, but their fundamental principles are not so mystifying, at least if you've come this far. They work on the principle that neat petrol, though it does burn fiercely — as you will have discovered if you've ever unwisely tried lightly a bonfire with some — is mostly all show. If you try sparking neat petrol in a car engine, what is most likely to happen is that the liquid will stop the spark from sparking at all. This condition, which you can sometimes inadvertently achieve by trying to start your car for too long with the choke full out, is known as 'flooding'. Petrol needs to form a vapour of fine droplets in air to be most effective as a source of heat energy and therefore of power at the wheels. What's more, the proportion of petrol to air is critical to making the engine run well. As with the ignition timing, this arrangement needs to change from time to time to suit the running conditions of the car.

The device that governs this, and effectively acts as a meter for the fuel supply, is the carburettor. Although some sophisticated modern cars have electronically-governed fuel-metering called **petrol injection**, a carburettor linked to an accelerator or throttle pedal in the car is the most common system.

In the more usual arrangement, your foot is connected to a simple flap in the tube down which air and petrol pass to the combustion chambers. This is called the **choke tube**. It abruptly reduces the size of the air passage into the engine, causing the air speed to quicken so that a suction effect is exerted on the fuel supply. The choke tube then spreads out into a number of pipes which lead to each cylinder — the **inlet manifold**. (In engineering, anything that divides the supply of liquid or gas from a single source to a number of outlets, or vice versa, is called a manifold.) Mounted on the air-intake side of the accelerator flap (or **throttle butterfly**) is the carburettor itself.

All carburettors are founded on the following essentials:

★ **A fuel reservoir** that acts like a cistern in your household plumbing, and both stores incoming fuel from the tank and maintains the correct level of fuel inside the carburettor. This reservoir is called the **float chamber** because a metal or plastic float inside acts like a ballcock, and cuts off the incoming fuel supply when the correct level is reached.

★ **A system of jets**, which are simply brass fittings with very small drillings in them, and which 'meter' the quantity of fuel or air that can be sucked through by the vacuum created by the descending pistons. You can figure out from this that the designer, by varying the sizes of the apertures by minute amounts, can alter the quantities of petrol and air that the carburettor can supply to the engine. Similarly, if the apertures are reduced in size or blocked entirely by dirt in the fuel supply, the performance of the car will deteriorate or disappear — this is a common kind of roadside breakdown that most motorists will have experienced to their exasperation.

PRINCIPLE OF CARBURETTORS

Because of the partial vacuum in the air intake, air pressure forces fuel from reservoir to intake via spray tube.

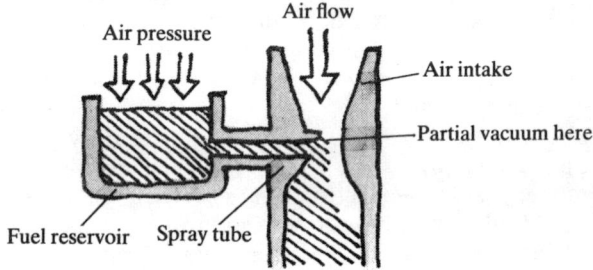

SIMPLE DOWNDRAUGHT CARBURETTOR

When the level in the float chamber drops, the float falls to allow more fuel in from petrol pump.

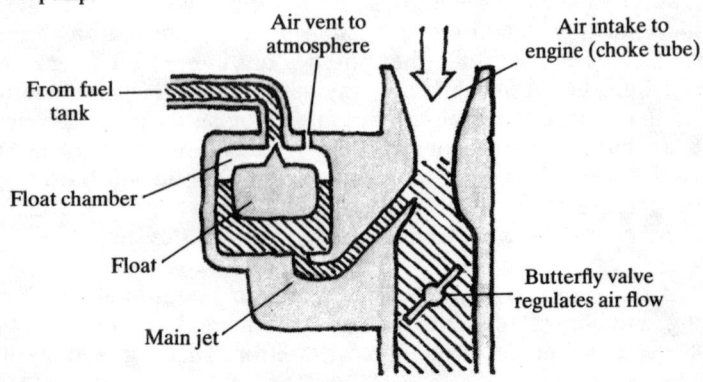

★ **A rich-mixture system** or 'choke'. This is a method, either automatically or manually administered, for greatly increasing the proportion of petrol to air to start the car and to drive it when cold. Petrol needs to evaporate in air to be combustible — it does this easily when the engine's hot, but is reluctant when it's cold. To ensure that there is enough petrol to gain a useful amount of evaporation, the mixture has to be 'enriched' when the engine is cold, but once the engine has reached its proper temperature, the choke either cuts out, or is put out of action by the driver. Chokes work either by opening up the aperture of the fuel supply so that more gets in, or (and this is the method that actually justifies the use of the word 'choke') by restricting the air intake, so that the proportion of petrol in the mix is higher.

As with the ignition system, although these are the basics, it isn't as simple as all that. The problem is that at high engine speeds more petrol is sucked in by the engine than it strictly needs, and at low speeds too little comes through to keep the engine going.

Carburettor designs to cope with this have fallen into two distinct types. In the most common variant, a sophisticated network of subsidiary jets is used to ensure that the device remains sensitive to

VARIABLE-JET CARBURETTOR

On full throttle engine sucks air from suction chamber. Piston assembly rises, drawing needle from jet, thus increasing flow of fuel.

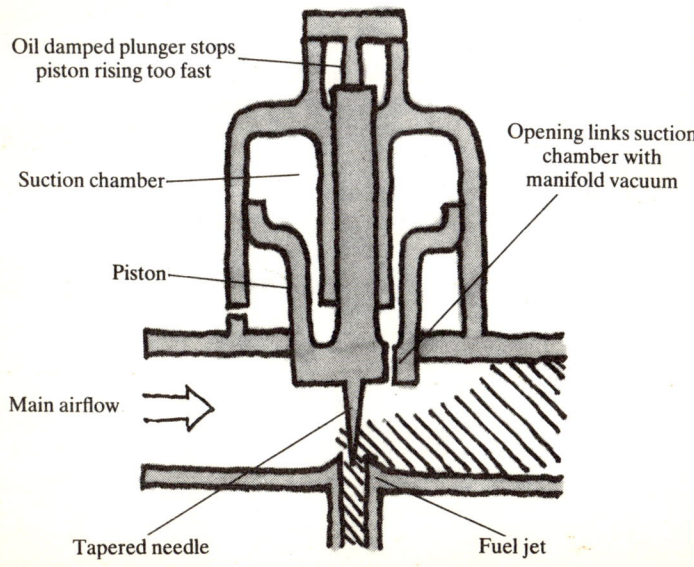

Oil damped plunger stops piston rising too fast

Opening links suction chamber with manifold vacuum

Suction chamber

Piston

Main airflow

Tapered needle

Fuel jet

the driving conditions — this is called 'fixed-jet' type, because the air passages are fixed sizes and the mechanism is designed to cut in some and cut out others according to the air speeds through the unit. In the 'variable-jet' carburettor — a much simpler design (adopted by the SU company, and by Zenith-Stromberg) — there is one central petrol jet, the size of which is varied by the rising and falling of a tapered needle within it. Some carburettors are even made up of two smaller units linked together, one for zero-to-mid-range throttle openings, the other taking over at higher speeds.

SERVICE INDUSTRY — THE ENGINE'S ANCILLARIES

LUBRICATION

Early engines were lubricated by a kind of drip-feed, but since they tended to run very slowly anyway the shortcomings of this system were not catastrophic. As improved engine design produced better performance, the need for more effective lubrication developed with it. The use of oil is designed to keep metal surfaces that meet at a point of considerable friction (bearings and pistons and cylinder walls particularly) slightly apart as the lubricating film rubs between them.

Engine oil is carried in a tank (or **sump**) bolted to the underside of the crankcase. A suction pump immersed in the oil draws it up into a network of passageways and apertures that pressure-feed it to the bearings, and the splashing of the oil as it escapes from the sides of the bearings coats the cylinder walls and protects them and the pistons. The camshaft and valve gear are similarly lubricated via small tubes supplied from the pump. Oil constantly drains back into the sump and is recirculated. Most engines have a **filter** somewhere in the system, which is simply a metal drum with a paper filter inside, to trap dirt carried around in the oil, which might otherwise accelerate deterioration of the bearings and moving parts. Replacement of the filter is a crucial part of engine servicing.

COOLING

The heat generated through the burning of fuel inside the engine is considerable. Without some means of dispersing it, the hottest parts (such as the exhaust valves) would rapidly burn, and the bearings and pistons deteriorate. Some cars are air-cooled, which means that a large fan simply blows cold air over the surfaces, and their crankcases are usually 'finned' to improve heat dispersal. The more usual arrangement, though, is that the cylinders, valves and combustion chambers are surrounded by hollow sections filled with water. This water is propelled around the system by a pump usually driven by a rubber belt off the crankshaft (the **fan belt**) and circulated through a **radiator**.

Water passing through the radiator is cooled down by a fan — which may be powered by a separate electric motor or attached to the front of the pump and run off the crankshaft — and also by the flow of cold air through it when the car is in motion. Hot water in the system can also be diverted to the car's heater, which is a smaller radiator inside the vehicle. To help the car warm up more quickly from cold, a **thermostat** is installed in the pipe between the water pump and the radiator. When the water is cold, the thermostat is shut and prevents circulation through the radiator that would otherwise keep it cool. As it warms up, the thermostat opens and full circulation occurs.

The only drawback with the water-cooling system, of course, is that in very cold weather it will freeze up, with much the same effect as such a thing will have in your household plumbing. In the case of the car, the radiator may split, or, even worse, the cylinder head or crankcase may crack. To avoid this, a chemical variant of alcohol is mixed with the cooling water to lower the freezing point (**antifreeze**).

One last consideration arises over the engine, which we've more or less taken apart and put back together again. It's possible to see from the previous descriptions how the movement of the pistons and crankshaft, and consequently of the camshaft, makes everything else happen in its proper order. The descending pistons create a vacuum which sucks in the fuel in proportions determined by the aperture sizes in the carburettor. The rotating crankshaft runs the fan belt and thus the water pump and fan at one end, and the gearwheels or pulley belt that turns the camshaft at the other. The camshaft in turn co-ordinates the actions of the valves, the distributor, the oil pump, and sometimes the fuel pump too. But if this is all well and good when the engine's happily firing away, pedalling its Otto cycle for all it's worth, one question remains:

What gets it going in the first place?

As we saw from the thumbnail sketch of motoring history, the answer to this used to be simply the attentions of the chauffeur or the hardy motorist, rotating the crankshaft by hand with a crank-handle until a stray spark managed to ignite the mixture thus drawn in and get the thing running by itself. This undignified procedure was mercifully replaced early on in the century by the electric self-starter. This is simply a powerful electric motor, bolted on to the side of the crankcase, and powered by the car's battery.

When you turn the key, the starter spins round. A sliding gear-wheel on one end of it moves down to engage with a ring of teeth around the circumference of the engine's flywheel, that heavy metal disc bolted to the crankshaft. When the teeth engage, the starter spins the crankshaft, and all the ancillaries and subsystems of the engine start going about their business, vaporizing fuel, opening and closing valves, sending sparks into cylinders. With a bit of luck, a spark soon catches a cylinderful of compressed fuel and the engine starts running by itself. Once the engine is rotating faster than the starter, the former pushes the sliding gearwheel out of mesh with the flywheel (if this didn't happen the engine would 'drive' the starter faster than is healthy for it, and burn it out), and you let go of the key and head for the hills.

THE STARTER MOTOR

The starter is bolted to rear of engine block.

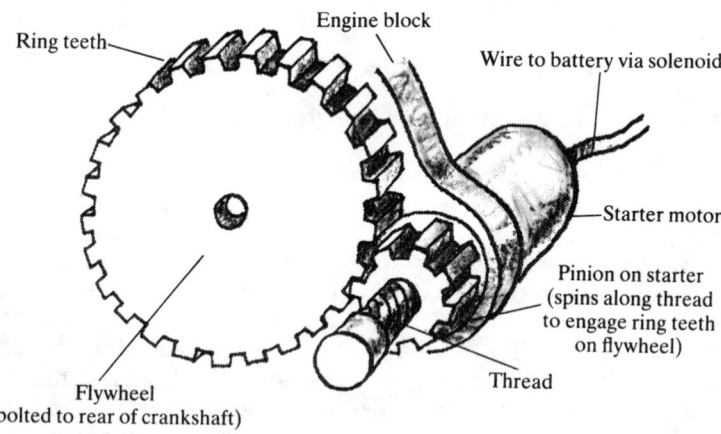

Ring teeth

Engine block

Wire to battery via solenoid

Starter motor

Pinion on starter
(spins along thread
to engage ring teeth
on flywheel)

Thread

Flywheel
(bolted to rear of crankshaft)

Diesel engines. Despite cheap fuel the relatively low performance and high noise of diesels made them unsaleable for private use for years. Lately, advances in technology have made them more attractive. In the diesel engine, the conventional ignition system is done away with and **compression ignition** used instead. Simply compressing hot air under the action of the piston and then pumping fuel oil in is sufficient to ignite the mixture.

Two-stroke engines. Petrol engines such as those used on motor-bikes can also be made to do away with the conventional Otto cycle and to work on two strokes instead of four. Valves are done away with, and holes or 'ports' in the cylinder wall, covered or uncovered according to the position of the piston, are deployed instead.

THE SOLENOID

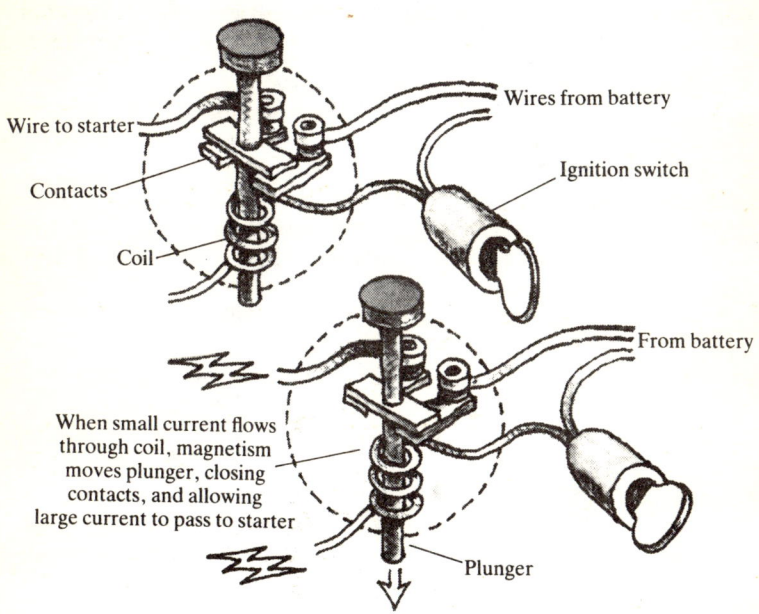

Wire to starter

Wires from battery

Contacts

Ignition switch

Coil

From battery

When small current flows through coil, magnetism moves plunger, closing contacts, and allowing large current to pass to starter

Plunger

TRANSMISSION

But what's the point of power if you can't use it?

So far what we have is a moderately efficient internal combustion engine, sitting at the front or back of the car, mounted with its line of pistons parallel to the roadwheels or at right angles to them. But you can't simply find a way of hooking the spinning crankshaft to an axle and blithely drive off. If you think about it, the reasons are not that astonishing:

★ **Moving from rest**. You, and your passengers, want the car to accelerate gently from rest. Always supposing it were possible to start an engine that was linked directly to the roadwheels, you could find that as soon as the engine fired, the car would be off down the road like a hare on a dog-track and the occupants of the car would probably have suffered severe concussion into the bargain. In practice, the engine needs to be detached from the roadwheels when it is being started — so that the crankshaft can be rotated at speed without the car trying to go anywhere — and also when it is about to be driven, so that the power from the crankshaft can be *gently* applied to the wheels and allow the vehicle to make a dignified departure.

★ **Adjusting power output to road conditions**. A car engine, particularly a modern car engine, can be very powerful, despite its relatively lightweight and small-scale moving parts, but there are limitations to its power. Most of these are bound up with the description *internal* combustion engine. That means that the car burns its fuel in the same space in which the hot expanding gas is applied to the piston — and it is the action of the pistons that make almost everything else on the engine work.

The effect of this on a car attempting to go uphill, for instance, is immediately striking. As it hits the incline, the engine starts to run more slowly. However far you depress the accelerator, the action of the engine is against you. The piston speed is slowing down, so the air speed through the carburettor slows down, and the whole process becomes a vicious circle. In a steam engine, for instance (an external combustion engine), this doesn't happen because the hot gas isn't being produced inside the piston space but is forced into it from an external boiler. As long as the steam pressure is high enough in the boiler, it will go on forcing its way into the cylinders and push the vehicle uphill however slowly the driving wheels are rotating.

So the car needs a means of rotating the roadwheels at very low speeds while the engine itself is running fast, for hill-climbing, and for allowing the roadwheels to spin quickly at relatively lower engine speeds, for cruising on a level surface. It also needs a device to make it drivable in reverse as well as forwards.

★ **Linking the power to the roadwheels**. This has to be done in such a way that the wheels of the car can still be sprung to avoid road-shocks, and that the vehicle can turn corners without upsetting the drive to the wheels.

The solutions to these three problems all involve terms you're bound to know:

- **Moving from rest**. The device that makes this possible is the **clutch**.

- **Adjusting power according to the road conditions**. The solution to this is a **gearbox**.

- **Linking power to the roadwheels**. This is performed via the **differential** or **final drive**.

All these gadgets need a brief run-down of their customs and practices if you're to understand what your friendly mechanic means when explaining why one or other of them needs expensive replacement.

THE CLUTCH

What you know about the clutch is almost certainly that it's a pedal you're taught to depress when you want to change gear, and bring up delicately when you want to set off into the world at large. Maybe even that when it's 'gone', your car and you sit miserably by the side of the road waiting for the tow truck, or at best you take off from rest like a frog on amphetamines or climb hills at a speed that would make walking preferable.

The hidden story of what happens after that pedal you know so well disappears into the carpets is that it links via a cable, a rod or a hydraulic system to a gadget bolted on to the face of the crankshaft flywheel. This is the true 'clutch', and the bit you're familiar with is merely the clutch pedal.

The clutch is just a sandwich, to put it simply. Moreover, it's a sandwich in which the ingredients can be squeezed hard when they need to be, and released so that they barely contact each other when they don't need to be. Look at the sketch to get the hang of the principle.

Remember that the point of the clutch is to link the **engine**, which provides the power, to the **gearbox**, which is able to turn the roadwheels at different speeds in relation to the engine speed, to suit the inclination of the road and the load on the vehicle.

With that in mind, consider the clutch again. It's a large soup plate-like device almost as big as the flywheel and fastened to it by a ring of bolts. Inside it is a steel disc, sprung against the interior of the soup plate by powerful coil springs or by an equally powerful diaphragm. The important thing to remember about this component, the clutch **pressure plate**, is that it's bolted to the crankshaft via the flywheel and rotates with it.

Into the centre of the flywheel comes a spindle from the gearbox, the unit to which the power from the engine has to be diplomatically introduced if severe communication breakdowns are not to occur. Although the spindle revolves in a bearing in the centre of the flywheel, it is independent of it. But fastened to the spindle, and thus in train with the gearbox, is another disc, this time made of an asbestos-like material. This is the clutch **centre plate**, and makes the 'filling' of our sandwich, between the flywheel and the pressure plate. Remember that the pressure plate is working for the engine, and the centre plate is working for the gearbox. When the sandwich isn't compressed, the two discs thus revolve independently of each other.

This is what is happening when your foot presses the clutch pedal to the floor. The 'sandwich' is slack, and the engine can spin freely, or you can rev it up as fast as you like, without the gearbox being affected at all.

When you release the pedal, the mechanism (**release bearing**) that is holding the pressure plate back against its springs withdraws, and allows the springs to push the pressure plate hard against the centre plate. Trapped against the face of the flywheel, it is thus

CLUTCH ENGAGED   CLUTCH DISENGAGED

All shaded components driven by engine

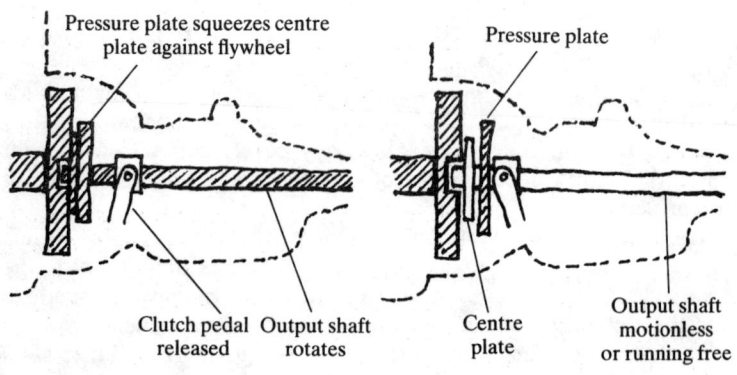

Pressure plate squeezes centre plate against flywheel

Pressure plate

Clutch pedal released

Output shaft rotates

Centre plate

Output shaft motionless or running free

CLUTCH OPERATION

Flywheel and clutch cover (including
springs, release levers and pressure plate)
revolve together as unit

Input shaft
and clutch plate
running free

Input
shaft
driven

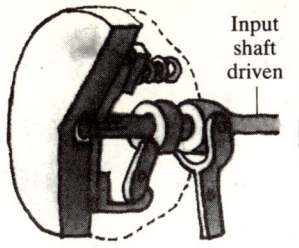
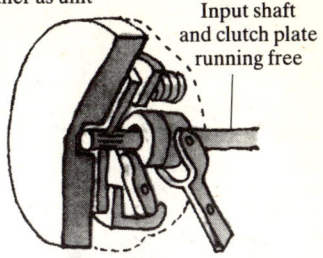

Clutch pedal released, clutch
plate engaged (pressed
against flywheel by springs)

Clutch pedal depressed, clutch
plate disengaged (thrust
bearing acts via release levers
to draw pressure plate from flywheel)

forced to rotate in sympathy with it. In this condition, the engine
drives the gearbox. But if you *slowly* release the pressure on the
clutch pedal, the pressure plate equally slowly insinuates itself
against the gearbox's centre plate. The friction face of the asbestos
surface begins revolving, slowly at first and slipping, but gradually
catching up with the engine speed until they're revolving together.
Done properly, this is what enables the car to move from rest with
chauffeur-like delicacy.

THE GEARBOX

So by means of the clutch we have been able to introduce the
engine's power to the gearbox, which offers the driver a choice of
roadwheel speeds in relation to the speed of the engine. These can
be manually selected by the driver in a car with a conventional
gear-shift, or the whole operation can be effected remotely in an
automatic gearbox — a far more complicated arrangement that
requires no clutch pedal.

In a conventional gearbox, the principle is exactly the same as the
one behind the gears you would find on a bicycle. For centuries,
humanity has practised methods of transforming limited amounts
of power (weedy primates attempting to shift massive rocks for
instance) in order to do disproportionately substantial work. The
principle has always been **leverage**. With gearwheels, if a small
wheel rotating fast is linked by a rope or a chain to a much larger
wheel, the latter will rotate more slowly but with greatly increased
leverage, or **torque**. The bigger the second wheel, the slower the

rotation, but the greater the power. The gearbox of a motor car permits the rotation of the engine's crankshaft to be linked to a choice of output wheels of different sizes, selected either by the driver or automatically. If the car is to climb a steep hill or to start from rest, the output wheel needs to be big, so the road-speed is slow but the torque is high. To run on the flat, the output wheel can be small, so that the rotational speed of the engine and that of the drive to the wheels might be more or less the same.

Gearboxes usually contain four forward speeds and one reverse, and sometimes five forward speeds. The most complicated feature of their design is that which enables the driver to shift from one gear to another while the car is in motion without creating uncool sound effects by crunching the spinning gearwheels against one another. Remember that although you depress the clutch to disengage the gearbox from the engine when changing gear, the gearwheels are still spinning even if they're not actually driven.

In early cars, it was up to the driver to judge by sound alone when the gear being sought for engagement was likely to be revolving at the right speed. Following the invention of **synchromesh**, the 'ambassadors' of the gearwheels, in the form of miniature clutch-like friction discs, would meet first and start rubbing together to balance up the speeds of the opposing components before any teeth attempted to mesh with each other. All this would be happening quickly, in the space of your moving the shift from one gear to another, but it made the difference between extremely nerve-wracking transportation and the kind of smooth and silent driving we're accustomed to today.

You don't really need to know much more about how a gearbox works than that, since few amateurs these days spend much of their lives taking such things apart. But for the curious, the sketch illustrates the way a gearbox goes through the motions.

The upper line of gears features the **primary shaft** at the clutch end, and the **mainshaft** or output shaft at the opposite end. First, second, third and fourth-speed gearwheels are all spinning on this upper line, but *independently* of one another, and free of the shafts they spin on. Any one of them can be **locked** to the mainshaft by a system of sliding hubs operated from the gear-shift. Whichever one you lock to the mainshaft is the gear you're driving in.

Below the mainshaft is a corresponding set of gears, but this time not spinning independently. In fact the lower shaft or **layshaft** is usually a solid piece of steel from which the gears have been cut *en bloc*. This is linked by a **constant mesh** pair of gears to the primary

TRANSMISSION PATH: FIRST GEAR

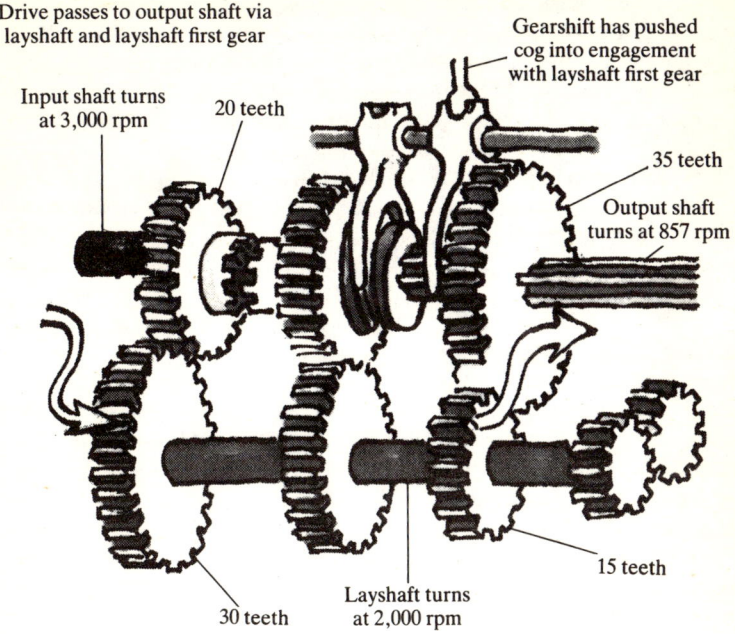

Drive passes to output shaft via layshaft and layshaft first gear

Gearshift has pushed cog into engagement with layshaft first gear

Input shaft turns at 3,000 rpm

20 teeth

35 teeth

Output shaft turns at 857 rpm

15 teeth

30 teeth

Layshaft turns at 2,000 rpm

shaft from the clutch. So when the engine is running, the entire layshaft is idling round at the same speed, and with it the gears on the mainshaft too (often with the exception of first, particularly on older cars). But if none of the upper gears spinning on their main-shaft is actually locked into engagement with it, then nothing happens at the output end and the gearbox is in **neutral**.

Once you lock one of the gears to the mainshaft by moving both the shift and, via a system of levers, the sliding locking hubs, then the revolving layshaft, driven by the engine, starts to turn the output shaft too. To start from rest, you engage first gear, and then move up through the other ratios when the car is under way.

Gearboxes are normally fairly reliable mechanisms and princi-pally just need a clean and robust transmission oil to run in, in which respect they're less trouble than engines, with all the regular maintenance of plugs, points and carburettors that the latter need. When gearboxes *do* wear, the bearings at either end of the box often get sloppy, which changes the way the gear teeth engage with one another. This will make the operation of the box noisier, and teeth on the gears may wear or chip. The sliding hubs that lock the wheels to the mainshaft may wear too, or even break up, making engagement noisier, or actually impossible. The shift mechanism itself may get slack. This or the hub wear may make the gears prone to jumping out of engagement. Usually the solution these days is to replace or rebuild the gearbox. We did hear an allegedly true story of a man arrested for driving backwards whilst inebriated who claimed he had been using this method for two years because the rest of the gearbox didn't work.

AUTOMATICS

From the standpoint of the average car-owner, getting involved in the intimacies of automatic gearboxes is more trouble than you need in one lifetime. Automatics are not trouble-prone in general, but when something does go wrong with them it tends to be expensive, and it tends to be work for a specialist. This has always been the case, but is especially so in contemporary automatic designs, which are often governed by sophisticated electronics.

As a working guide, a short summary of the workings of an automatic transmission is as follows:

★ **The clutch** does not exist on an automatic in the sense we described earlier. The substitute is a device called a **torque converter**, a hydraulic mechanism whereby the increasing speed of the engine as you accelerate the car from rest throws a reservoir of oil in the centre of the unit out towards the extremities of it under centrifugal force, and the drive is taken up smoothly by this means. Torque converters 'gear down' the engine of their own accord, so to some extent they act as substitute to fulfil the role of gears.

★ **The gearbox**. On automatics, such gears as there are mostly function on a slightly different principle, know as **epicyclic gearing**. Instead of the simple arrangement whereby two gearwheels of different sizes mesh with each other to change an input speed to an output speed, an input shaft drives a central **sunwheel**. Revolving around the circumference of this are a pair of small **planet wheels**. The entire collection in turn revolves *inside* a big ring with gear teeth on its inner surface, called an **annulus**. Different output ratios, and alteration of the drive from forward to reverse can be achieved according to whether the output mechanism carrying the planet wheels is locked stationary while the **annulus carrier** revolves, or whether the latter is locked and the former allowed to rotate. This locking and unlocking is achieved by friction mechanisms operated hydraulically. In the past, mechanical contraptions hooked to the accelerator would bring all this about, but latterly microcircuitry has been deployed instead.

FINAL DRIVE

Throughout this chapter we've been talking about almost everything to do with the actual propulsion of your motor car except the thing you most need it for — getting from A to B. How do all these other mechanisms on the machine finally get the roadwheels to turn round and get you rolling?

OK, you know what wheels are, or if you don't you won't have got this far. You're also likely to know that an axle is what joins a wheel to the object it's moving around, and that on primitive transport a single axle will have a wheel at each end.

On modern motor cars, while the principles are the same, the practice is different — for reasons of comfort, convenience and safety.

For a start, the roadwheels nowadays tend to be joined in a single, short axle attached to the 'box' of the motor car in a kind of sprung slide, so that the wheel and the axle together can rise and fall over bumps and holes in the road. Where a pair of wheels are fixed to each end of a single axle, this will also be sprung against the body of the car to absorb shocks.

Secondly, there must be a mechanism — usually deploying gears — whereby the power from the engine, via the clutch and gearbox, can be made to rotate the wheels. On most cars, only one pair of wheels is actually 'driven' — for years, these were the back ones, but since the 1960s the use of front-drive has become much more common. Some vehicles, such as jeeps, intended for more rugged use, even offer the option of driving all four wheels, which is helpful on rough or slippery terrain.

You might think, if you've followed us so far, that this would be a simple question of gearing the output shaft of the transmission to a gear on the axle and that's that. But there is, believe it or not, a problem:

When a car goes round a corner, the roadwheels nearest to the bend are rotating faster than the ones further away. So a special gearing system is necessary that allows the outer drive wheel to 'idle', while the inner one is screaming round the corner. A set-up with some similarities to the epicyclic gears we described earlier is used for this and is called a **differential** (usually referred to by dog end-chewing engineers as a 'diff'). As you can see from the drawing, the inner ends of the axles carrying the driven wheels have a pair a conical gears, called **bevel gears** attached to them. These two gears don't actually mesh directly with each other, but are linked by a pair of smaller gears (**pinions**).

HOW A DIFFERENTIAL UNIT WORKS

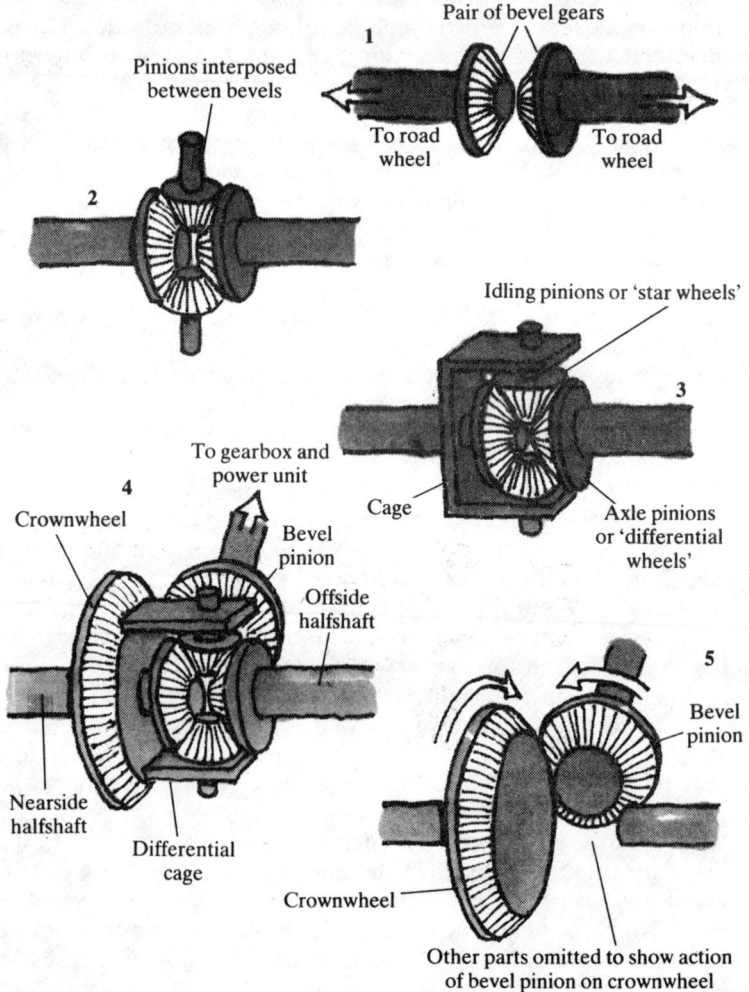

Pair of bevel gears

1

Pinions interposed between bevels

To road wheel

To road wheel

2

Idling pinions or 'star wheels'

3

To gearbox and power unit

Cage

Axle pinions or 'differential wheels'

4

Crownwheel

Bevel pinion

Offside halfshaft

5

Bevel pinion

Nearside halfshaft

Differential cage

Crownwheel

Other parts omitted to show action of bevel pinion on crownwheel

The pinions are carried in a fork or **cage**, bolted to the much bigger gearwheel (the **crownwheel**) that you see in the drawing. The crownwheel is driven by a bevel gear running from the gearbox and propelled by the engine. When the car is running in a straight line, the crownwheel thus rotates the differential cage, and with it the two pinions. As they perform their circuit, they drive the axle's bevel gears. But when one axle is rotating faster than the other, the pinions begin to rotate themselves to take up the difference.

The only other equipment the motor car needs to get its wheels rolling effectively is a method of conveying the drive to the wheels themselves that suits the layout of the car and takes account of steering and springing. If you think about it, the transfer of power from a transmission system to a wheel is fairly straightforward, simply using a straight tube or shaft (a **propeller shaft**). But it's not so simple if the wheels are going to be bumping up and down over road-shocks or turning from side to side to steer the car, as is the case if the front wheels are the driven ones.

UNIVERSAL JOINT

Forked ends of shafts pivot on 'spider'. Bearings reduce friction.

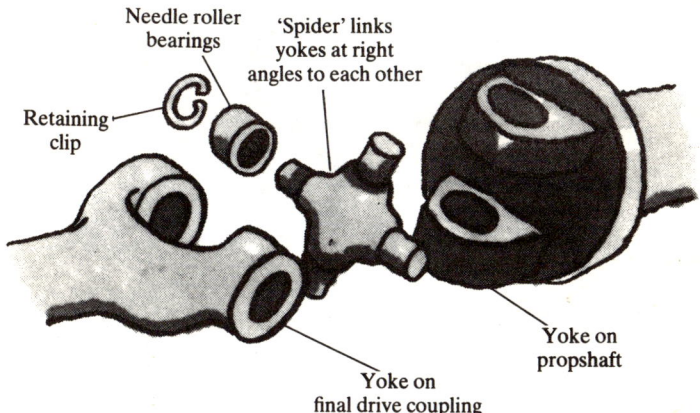

Needle roller bearings

'Spider' links yokes at right angles to each other

Retaining clip

Yoke on propshaft

Yoke on final drive coupling

Consequently all kind of sophisticated telescopic and universally-jointed devices have been developed to combine the need for rotational movement with up-and-down and side-to-side movement to cope with springing and steering. These gadgets may be known variously as **universal joints** or **driveshaft couplings** or **constant-velocity joints**, depending on the design of the car. Some of these components are quite sophisticated constructions involving ball-bearings and very accurate machining, which are not amenable to servicing and generally have to be replaced when they wear and become noisy.

So that's the way you get it going. What comes next is what you might call the way the motor car is socialized. How to keep it from hitting people and objects is the subject of the next chapter.

CONSTANT-VELOCITY JOINT

Normally used for drive shafts. Steel balls held in cage transmit drive from inner to outer socket.

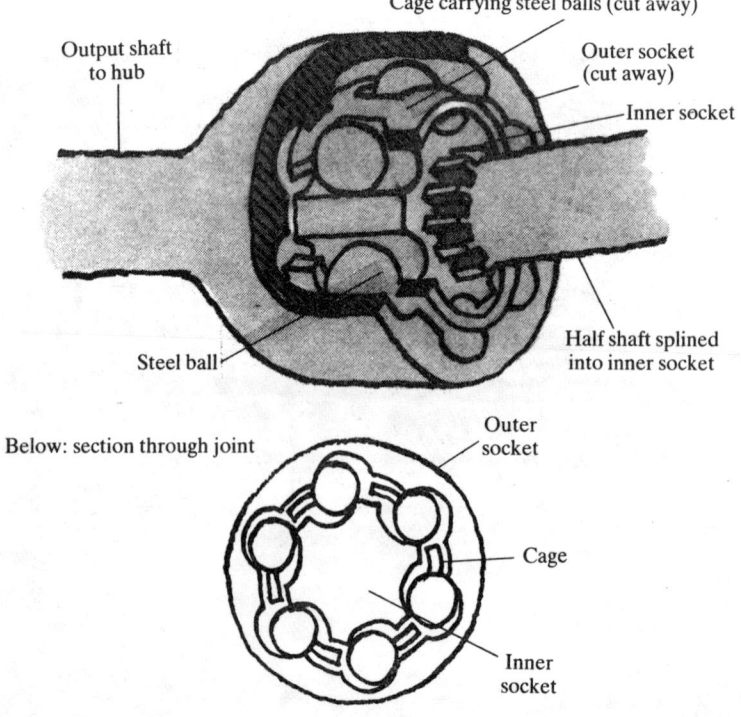

Cage carrying steel balls (cut away)

Output shaft to hub

Outer socket (cut away)

Inner socket

Half shaft splined into inner socket

Steel ball

Below: section through joint

Outer socket

Cage

Inner socket

3

MAKING TRACKS

'There's a lot of debate on this subject —
about what kind of car handles best. Some say a
front-engined car;
some say a rear-engined car. I say a rented car.
Nothing handles better than a rented car.
You can go faster, turn corners sharper and put the transmission
into reverse while going forward
at a higher rate of speed in a rented car than in any other kind.'
(P. J. O'Rourke, National Lampoon)

In the early days of motoring, not only were the creature comforts of the passenger primitive, to say the least, but the widespread alarm and fears for life and limb that accompanied the rise of the horseless carriage couldn't be wholly dismissed as the ravings of Luddites and neurotics. To deserve its place in society, the motor car needed to learn how to get around without demolishing its surroundings — to which end it had to be able to see and be seen after sundown, to make itself heard, to avoid obstacles and to be able to stop as well as go.

TYRES AND WHEELS

Early horse-drawn vehicles had wooden wheels with steel rims. Human beings travelling on such things needed to have their insides made of similar materials. The early motor car used solid rubber tyres, which were better, but not much. Charles Goodyear, an American inventor, took the first step towards an improvement of this situation in 1839 when he dreamed up the vulcanization process — heat treating a compound of rubber, lead and sulphur. Then, in 1888, John B. Dunlop, a British vet, developed a pneumatic tyre for use on bicycles, and the invention coincided perfectly with the volcanic eruption of the motor-car industry. But it wasn't until the 1940s that synthetic rubber began to satisfy the insatiable needs of the global motor industry, and dependence on the latex dribbling from trees in Malaya began to dwindle.

Drivers tend to take tyres for granted — so much so that until the introduction of the MOT test in Britain, many cars were driven on tyres in a hair-raising state. But not only is their role in safety and handling critical, it depends on a very small percentage of the tyre's actual surface area. Look at your car while it's parked and think about the minute area of the tyre touching the road at any one moment during the wheel's revolution. Those few square centimetres have to support the car, cushion bumps, and grip the road whilst accelerating, braking, cornering and driving in the wet or snow.

To this end, modern tyres are tough constructions. Rubber on the outside, they are usually reinforced with steel wire, and the rubber parts themselves may be made of several different compounds according to the part of the tyre they are intended for. The road-contacting part of the tyre is grooved to form a **tread** so that water can drain from the surface more quickly in wet weather, thereby improving adhesion. A minimum tyre-tread depth is now a legal requirement for motorists in many countries. The tyre is inflated with compressed air to a pressure that strikes a balance between the softness that improves ride comfort at low speed and the hardness that improves steering and reduces overheating of the tyre on long fast drives.

It's worth noting that the difference between two tyre types, **radial** and **cross-ply** tyres, has nothing to do with the pattern of the treads, as is sometimes supposed. The terms refer to the pattern of the reinforcing material inside the tyre — in the former arranged more or less straight from rim to rim, in the latter arranged diagonally. The greater structural strength of the radial has led it to supersede the cross-ply.

CROSS-PLY TYRES

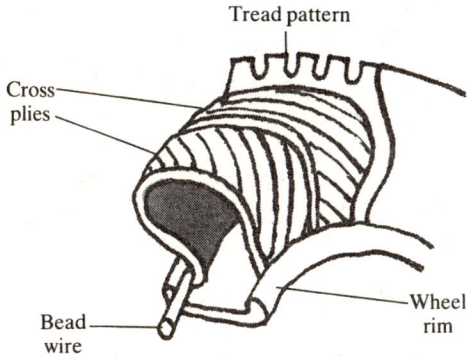

Tread pattern

Cross-plies

Bead wire

Wheel rim

RADIAL TYRES

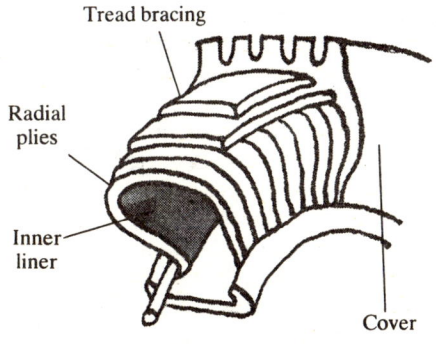

Tread bracing

Radial plies

Inner liner

Cover

WHEELS

Motor-car wheels used to be made like bicycle wheels — with a lattice-work of spokes connecting the hub to the wheel rim — and this method has remained popular as a symbol of motoring sportiness, although 'wires', as they are called, are increasingly being replaced by lightweight magnesium wheels, developed from racing practice. The standard alternative to wires has long been pressed-steel wheels, which are bolted to the hub assembly, whereas wire wheels are slid on to the hub and usually held in place by a single large nut.

A variety of handling problems, some of them minor, some of them severe and even a threat to safety, can be caused by one side of a tyre's being slightly heavier than the other — a condition impossible to diagnose until the tyre is inflated and fitted to the wheel, but easily remedied by the addition of small lead balance weights on the wheel rim. Wheel-balancing is a service offered by many tyre specialists. All manner of wobbles and odd handling characteristics can stem from neglecting this minor but vital attention.

SUSPENSION

In some highly-specialized motoring research departments, micro-technology is meeting automotive engineering to develop a breakthrough that most of us won't encounter until the 1990s. It's called 'active damping', also dubbed by one of its major developers, Volvo, 'computer control suspension'. It's a way of electronically 'reading' the road surface and adjusting the suspension in such a manner that the motorist is virtually oblivious of the usual in-car sensations of bumps, corners and sudden halts, or even of the difference between a motorway and an unmade road. The experience, according to those who have driven experimental vehicles with this facility, is nothing short of mind-boggling — and body-boggling too, for that matter.

All this is a very long way from the primitive cart-springs with which the motor industry not only launched itself on to the highways, but sustained its presence on them for several generations. **Leaf springs** are exactly what they say they are — a sandwich of several thin metal bars, heat-treated for elasticity and strength, which is bolted between the axle and the chassis or body and flexes with the axle's movements over obstacles. For years, this throwback to the earliest transport practice held sway in the motor industry too.

COIL SPRINGS

LEAF SPRINGS

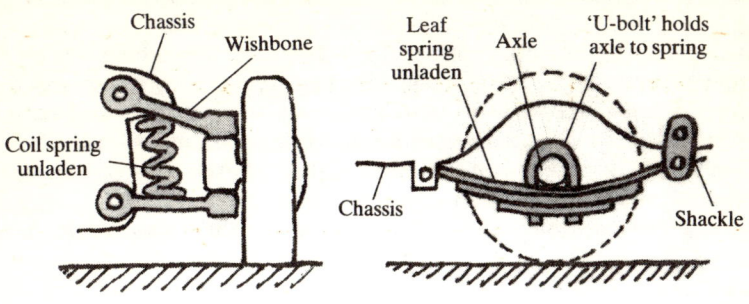

Chassis

Wishbone

Coil spring unladen

Leaf spring unladen

Axle

'U-bolt' holds axle to spring

Chassis

Shackle

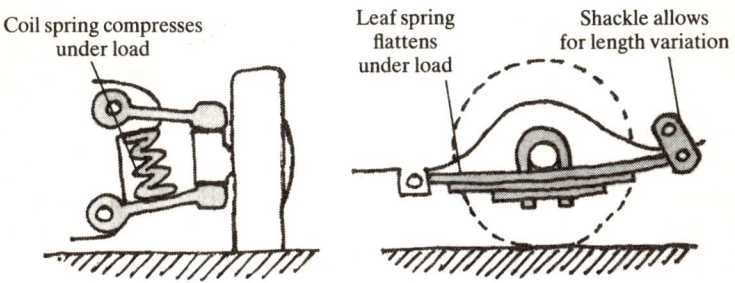

Coil spring compresses under load

Leaf spring flattens under load

Shackle allows for length variation

TORSION BARS

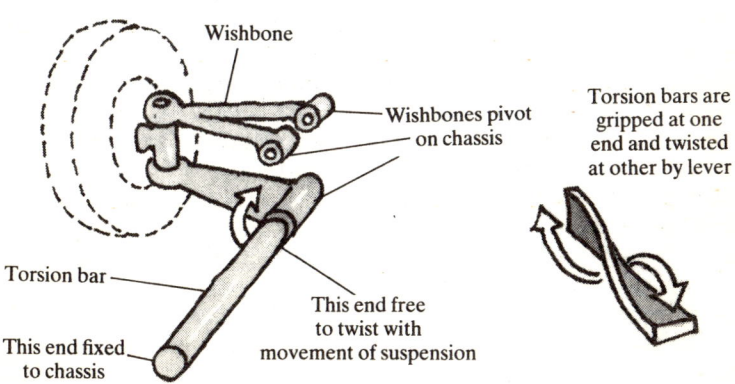

Wishbone

Wishbones pivot on chassis

Torsion bars are gripped at one end and twisted at other by lever

Torsion bar

This end free to twist with movement of suspension

This end fixed to chassis

Eventually a variant of what the public might nowadays more reasonably recognize as a spring — a coil of wire in a cylindrical shape — began to be used in suspension too, usually for the front wheels to begin with, but later used for all four. A less easily-recognizable variation of the coil spring that has also found favour is the **torsion bar**. This is a rod made of spring steel, which twists under load. Some manufacturers have preferred to use synthetic rubber, forming a conical spring that progressively stiffens as increasing load is put on it, and some, such as Citroën, have explored the use of compressed air or gas in suspension systems.

The problem with springs is that once they incur a shock from the road, they tend to go on rebounding for some time, an effect likely to make the occupants of the car feel that they are travelling on a wheeled trampoline rather than a masterpiece of 20th century engineering. The **shock-absorbers** are necessary to 'dampen' the rebound of the springs, and the term **dampers** is therefore a more strictly accurate description.

Imagine the problem. The spring goes 'twang' under the impact of a bump. The damper has to stop it continuing to vibrate like a tuning fork, without negating the effect of having a spring in the first place. In early cars, simple 'friction dampers' were used, in which two metal arms — one bolted to the spring, the other to the chassis — were pivoted together via the rubbing surfaces of a friction-faced, asbestos-derived material rather like that used for brake linings and clutches.

Dampers today operate **hydraulically**, which simply means that the extent to which an arm linked to the moving spring resists the spring's tendency to bounce is conditioned by how fast the small piston to which the arm is also linked can squeeze an oil called **hydraulic fluid** through a restricted aperture. In the **lever-arm** type, the vertical movement of the spring being cushioned moves a lever that activates two complementary pistons in the body of the damper — one for the bump, the other for the rebound. More usually found nowadays is the **piston** type, some of which are manufactured with provision for altering the settings so that different degrees of ride comfort are attainable.

Suspension systems are attached to the bodywork in a variety of ways. Once the traditional system using a pair of rigid axles had been superseded by that of independently springing the two front wheels (with a marked improvement in handling and steering) a variety of uses of levers came into play. You needed the roadwheel to be able to move vertically over bumps and holes, with the mechanism on which the roadwheel was mounted being able to accommodate springs and a damper and being itself 'hinged' at the top and the bottom to the motor-car's bodywork. Variations on these designs that permit independent suspension of the rear wheels have also become popular lately.

TELESCOPIC DAMPER

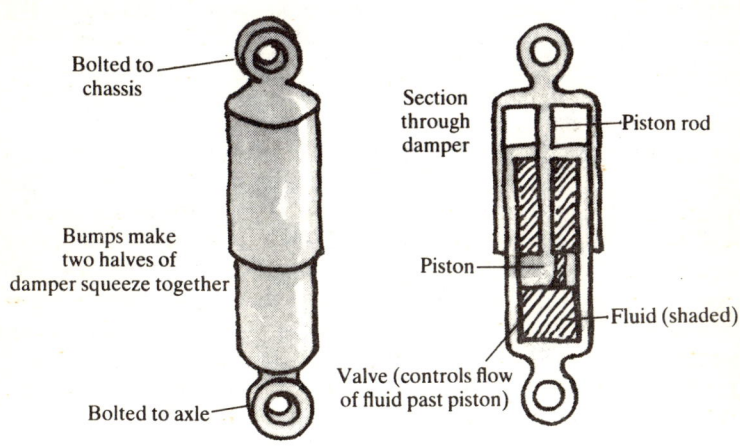

Bolted to chassis

Bumps make two halves of damper squeeze together

Bolted to axle

Section through damper

Piston rod

Piston

Fluid (shaded)

Valve (controls flow of fluid past piston)

STEERING

Early cars were steered, like boats, by means of a tiller. The steered wheels were on swivels, and linked to a simple lever that the driver moved from side to side. This was bearable in the days when an arthritic jogger with asthma could run faster than most motor cars, but it was of limited use as speeds increased.

A steering wheel was obviously more practical. But if the direction of travel was to be determined by the rotation of a wheel, then clearly a version of a gearing system would be necessary to convert the rotational movement into a side-to-side leverage that could alter the position of the roadwheels. And as cars advanced,

51

engineers also began to look for ways of isolating road-shocks from the steering wheel, reducing the effort needed to turn the steering wheel (particularly on large cars) and making the steering 'light' enough to be manageable at low road speeds and whilst parking, but not so light that the car would be positively dangerous at high speed.

As in the case of the transmission system, the right ratio of gears can be used to convert a moderate rotational effort (**torque**) into a much more substantial one at the output end. In earlier cars, where the suspension systems were of rather less than magic-carpet quality, a high degree of friction needed to be introduced into the steering gear to absorb bumps and shocks from the road. The designs that made this possible were eventually superseded as suspension systems improved. In the **rack-and-pinion** method, the rack is simply a toothed bar that runs across the front of the car, the ends of which are coupled to rods that move the roadwheels. A small gearwheel at the end of the steering column rotates as the steering wheel is turned and thus slides the bar from side to side. Other designs continue to be based on derivations of the earlier methods, using a type of spiral gear called a **worm** (see drawing) which rotates as the steering wheel does and moves a **rocker arm** in sympathy.

HOW STEERING WORKS

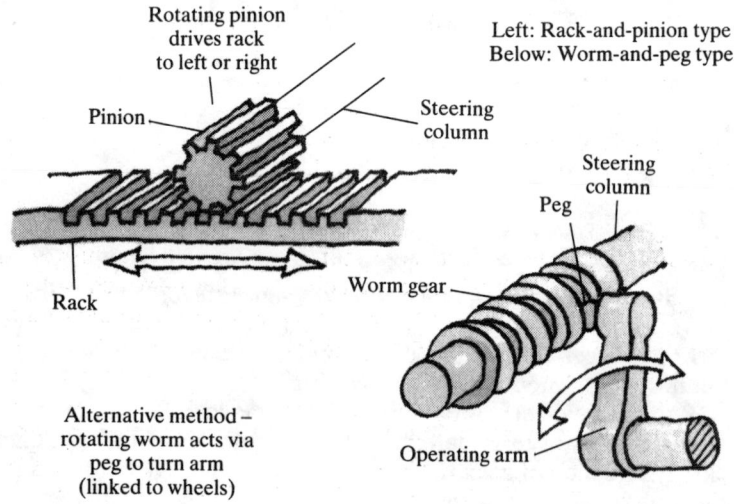

Rotating pinion
drives rack
to left or right

Left: Rack-and-pinion type
Below: Worm-and-peg type

Pinion

Steering
column

Steering
column

Peg

Worm gear

Rack

Alternative method –
rotating worm acts via
peg to turn arm
(linked to wheels)

Operating arm

There are considerable virtues in the fact that the steering is self-correcting — in other words, that the car will run in a straight line without much adjustment by the driver as long as the road is level. The angles at which the steering components are linked to one another is the crucial factor in this, so the arrangement is entitled the **steering geometry**. What counts is that the swivels on which the roadwheels themselves rotate are not actually vertical but tipped slightly backwards so that the lowest point of each swivel is further to the front of the vehicle than the centre point of the wheel. (The measurement of this is called the **castor angle**.) Additionally, viewed from the front of the car, the roadwheels are angled slightly from the vertical, with the top either tipped outwards (**camber angle**) or, more recently, tipped inwards (**negative camber**). They may also be splayed in or out in relation to the horizontal plane of the car (referred to as **toe-in** and **toe-out**).

All this geometry is necessary to ensure that the car is as manageable on the road as it can be. If you ever read road tests of cars, you may find references to characteristics such as 'understeer' and 'oversteer'. The tendencies denoted by these terms are all related to whatever compromises the manufacturers have settled for in setting up the steering gear. **Understeer** refers to the condition whereby the driver has to make extra effort to keep the car on course in a turn, and is caused by the steered wheels drifting further sideways (because of tyre flexibility) than the rear ones. If, on the other hand, the rear wheels drift further sideways than the front ones (**oversteer**), then unless this is corrected the car will tend to go out of control. Proper consideration to the camber angle, particularly, will increase the cornering power of the tyres. On some cars, the steering geometry is adjustable, and where this is the case it is vital to have it serviced, for reasons that should be obvious.

BRAKES

Considering how sophisticated motor cars have become over the years, the fundamental principle behind brakes — which is that of jamming something against drums of discs attached to the rotating roadwheels and slowing them down by friction — seems rather primitive. But that is what continues to happen, and although the principle is brutal enough, the systems that enable it to work certainly have grown much smarter as cars have evolved, with corresponding advances in road safety.

The ability of a car to pull up depends not only on its brakes but also on its tyres, and on the condition of the road. Brake design takes into account the fact that tyres exert their best grip just before they slide, so sophisticated braking systems found on some cars today have a built-in mechanism to release the brakes if the wheels do begin to lose grip and then to reapply them once adhesion is restored. Without such a mechanism, a driver making an emergency stop (particularly in the wet) can lose control of the car unless using the technique of slightly easing the braking effort to allow the wheels to grip again.

For years, **drum brakes** dominated the art of stopping motor cars in their tracks. The arrangement, as you can see from the drawing, is one whereby the roadwheel rotates on a **hub** in which ball-bearings keep friction on the spinning wheel down to a minimum. Screwed to the hub is a cast-iron **drum** which spins with it. The stationary part of the fitting is mounted either on the rear-axle mechanism, or on the steering swivel if at the front of the car. Fitted to this device is a pair of **brake shoes**, crescent-shaped components with a facing made of a hard-wearing friction material. These pivot in response to pressure on a brake pedal inside the car, so they can be pushed out to rub against the inside of the rotating drum if the brakes are being applied, or pulled back by return springs so that they're free of the drum when the brakes are not being applied.

The tendency of the revolving brake-drum to 'wrap' the lower shoe closer to itself and push the upper one away if revolving clockwise is also used in brake design to increase braking effect without requiring superhuman pressure on the pedal, and either self-adjusting or manually adjusted cams can alter the position of the shoe in relation to the drum to compensate for wear on the friction material.

In early cars, the means by which the pedal pressure exerted leverage on the shoes were rods or cables. Hydraulic brakes came into more or less general use after the last war, whereby a system of small-bored tubes leads to each wheel, fed from a central reservoir and a cylinder (**master cylinder**) with a piston in it, positioned somewhere not too far from the location of the brake pedal itself. The driver's effort on the brake moves the piston in the master cylinder, squeezes fluid out along the pipes and into smaller cylinders (**wheel cylinders**) mounted between the brake shoes. The tubes leading from the static bodywork to the steered and sprung roadwheels naturally have to become flexible sections at that point, to avoid breakages, lost fluid and accidents. The incoming fluid moves pistons in these cylinders, and pushes the shoes into contact with the drum.

THE BRAKING SYSTEM

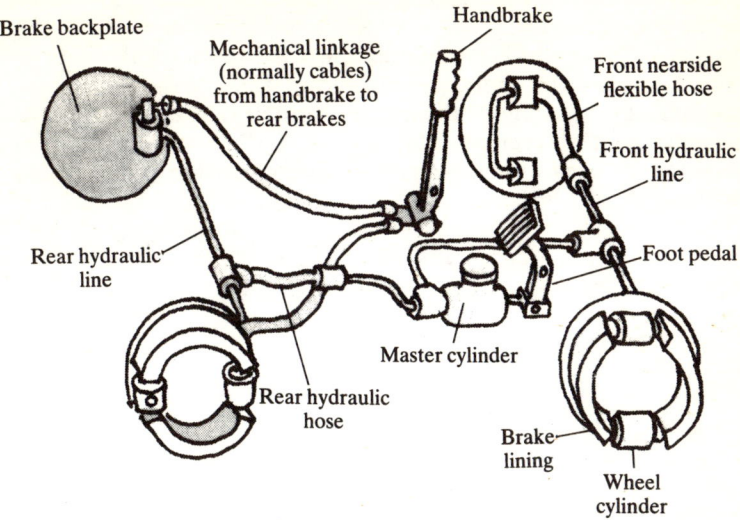

Brake backplate

Mechanical linkage
(normally cables)
from handbrake to
rear brakes

Handbrake

Front nearside
flexible hose

Front hydraulic
line

Rear hydraulic
line

Foot pedal

Master cylinder

Rear hydraulic
hose

Brake
lining

Wheel
cylinder

ACTION OF MASTER AND WHEEL CYLINDERS

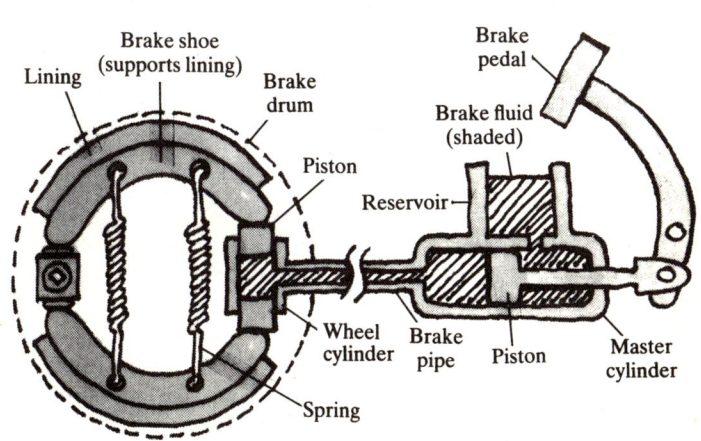

Lining

Brake shoe
(supports lining)

Brake
drum

Brake
pedal

Brake fluid
(shaded)

Piston

Reservoir

Wheel
cylinder

Brake
pipe

Piston

Master
cylinder

Spring

Disc brakes, which have increasingly superseded drums, simply consist of an iron disc spinning with the wheel instead of a drum. In place of the shoe mechanism there is a **calliper**, which is more or less a jaw that can clamp a pair of friction faces (pads) on to the disc by hydraulic pressure. The disc brake, not being enclosed, disperses heat much more efficiently than the drum. Heat tends to lead to the braking effort 'fading' and partly because of this disc brakes have become popular, even on cheaper cars. At the very least, discs are likely to be used at the front of the car where the need for high braking effort is greatest.

DISC BRAKES

Section through brake assembly (below) shows pads being forced against disc by hydraulic pressure . . .

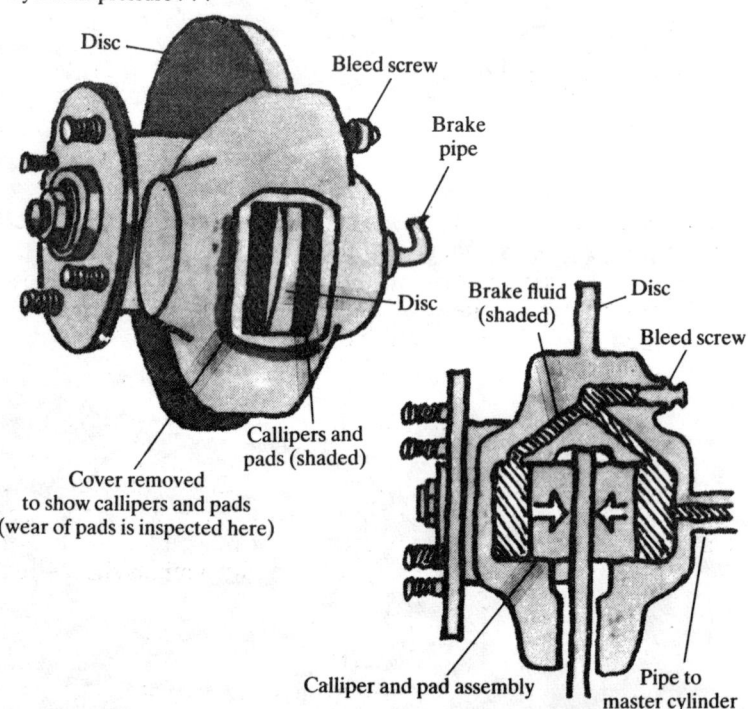

Disc

Bleed screw

Brake pipe

Disc

Brake fluid (shaded)

Disc

Bleed screw

Callipers and pads (shaded)

Cover removed to show callipers and pads (wear of pads is inspected here)

Calliper and pad assembly

Pipe to master cylinder

A **parking brake** or handbrake, which stops the car running away when left stationary, is also always a feature of the braking system. Hand-operated, it is usually linked by rods or cables to one pair of the roadwheels, generally the rear ones.

ELECTRICS

As we established when dealing with the ignition system and the starter, a motor car's electrical components are supplied from a storage battery, with the 'return' flow of current being conducted through the metalwork of the car itself, since the voltage is sufficiently low not to fry the occupants.

A car battery simply follows the school-physics principle of chemically storing electricity between two electrodes immersed in acid. The electricity can be generated either externally (the battery being charged from a modified mains supply) or from a small generator driven off the engine of the car, usually using the fan belt that also drives the water pump. The generator or **dynamo** just does what an electric motor does but the other way round. Revolving a wire coil between magnets will generate a current, just as passing a current into such a construction will make it revolve. Modified dynamos called **alternators** are now in much more common use, and they have the virtue of being compact and light, yet able to supply more current at lower engine speeds. Now that modern in-car heating and de-misting systems have become so effective, but also so current-consuming, the advantages of the generator have become clear.

Control mechanisms are needed in the charging circuit to deal with variations in the engine's speed. At very low revs, the generator may not produce as much as the 12 volts that most modern batteries are rated at. But if it produces less than battery voltage, the battery will try to drive it like a motor rather than the dynamo supply the battery. A cut-out is thus incorporated so that the connection between the two will be broken when this happens, and there are also regulatory mechanisms to prevent too high a battery charging rate (which can overheat the battery) or over charging (which dries out the battery fluid). Fashions have changed over the years regarding which side of the battery is treated as 'live' and which is the earth. On most modern cars, the negative pole of the battery (often colour-coded green and with a minus sign beside it) is earthed to the body.

LIGHTING

After sunset, the car has to be able to see in the dark, and other people have to be able to see it coming. Two small white lights at the front and two red ones at the rear, plus a light to illuminate the number plate at the back, are the legal requirements for the second stipulation. For finding its way around, the car is fitted with headlamps, which have to be capable of being used at their full strength and also on a **dipped** or reduced beam to avoid dazzling oncoming traffic. This trick is generally performed by means of **double-filament** bulbs, the main-beam light coming from the central filament, the dip from a second filament set slightly off-centre in the bulb. This is a marked improvement on the arrangement in the 1920s, whereby the entire body of the headlamp was tipped downwards by a lever on the dashboard marked 'pull smartly'. Some headlamps, instead of using separate bulbs, are **sealed-beam** units — the whole headlamp is the 'bulb', and if it goes everything has to be replaced.

OTHER ELECTRICAL COMPONENTS

Electrics are also used to signal changes in direction, via flashing amber lights, to signal braking to drivers behind, via very bright red lights at the rear, and to power horns. The electrical system also has to run windscreen-wipers, heater and de-mister fans and sometimes engine-cooling fans, and generally is obliged to perform a great deal of work.

Cables to all the various bits and pieces of a motor car that require electricity are grouped together in a spaghetti-like concoction called the **loom** or **harness**. In order that car electricians be spared visits to the asylum, the cables are supplied in a variety of different colours. Which colours are connected to what is recorded on a wiring diagram supplied by the car manufacturer. Fuses like the fuses in your house are also included somewhere in the wiring system — these are usually glass or plastic cartridges carrying a thin piece of wire which acts as a bridge in the circuit that's being protected by the fuse. If the circuit gets too hot because something's wrong with it, the fuse wire melts and disconnects the supply before the problem can severely damage the component or start a fire.

INSTRUMENTS

The only instrument on a car required by law is one that tells you if you're exceeding the speed limits. However, it's useful to have others — such as those that can warn you if you're running out of fuel or if your generator isn't charging the battery, and those that can tell you if your engine's about to expire. Current, oil-pressure and overheating warnings usually take the form of lights that come on if there's a problem, though gauges are sometimes fitted to cars in addition to the fuel gauge, which is more or less universal. They include a water-temperature gauge, an oil-pressure gauge (which provides a useful forewarning against wear in the engine bearings), and an ammeter, which measures current flowing in or out of the battery, and can tell you when the battery is in need of a recharge off the car.

SAFETY

Today's cars are as safe as they have ever been. But as the sticker in the back of one declared — 'designed by computer, built by robots, driven by a moron' — the human beings controlling them are as fallible as ever, even if road accident casualties aren't significantly higher than they were 50 years ago.

Every year, the manufacturers come out with newer and better safety features — anti-skid brakes, collapsible steering wheels, specially reinforced bodywork, computer warnings of impending failure. But some safety basics are now more or less standard. **Safety glass** is used on all modern cars, either containing a plastic laminate which stops it splintering, or toughened in a manner that makes it break into blunt chippings rather than shards. **Safety harnesses** are now standard in Britain, and increasingly common are anti-burst locks, which are designed to prevent doors opening as the body distorts in a crash.

4

CHANCING YOUR ARM

'The clutch was so stiff that the effort needed to
depress it left one standing up with the nape of the neck
pressed against the roof and one's teeth
wrapped around the rear-view mirror.
Moving the gearstick was
like pushing a parking meter around and the brakes
wouldn't have stopped a pram.
Then it rained and gradually I became aware that
my knees were wet. My friend nodded. "Yes," he said.
"It does that." '
(Alexander Frater in Punch)

Cars and houses, goes the truism, are the two biggest investments most people make in a lifetime. For all that, impulse and whim play a very large part in what people eventually go for. This can be the kind of choice you make in haste and repent at leisure, when you find, for instance, that the spares for your dream car cost a fortune or take months to obtain, that the petrol consumption is horrendous, or that on wet roads it handles like a toboggan. Not that falling in love with the styling or the paintwork should be banished from your thoughts. It just makes sense to weigh it up with all the longer-term considerations and to come to a decision based on some sort of logic and not rush to a conclusion because the vendor is peering at a wrist-watch and stamping irritably about. It's nothing compared with the irritation likely to be occasioned in your household if the car turns out to be a turkey, particularly when it comes to trying to get rid of it.

These are the primary considerations when you are working out what model you're after. Much of this information you'll be able to glean from the motoring magazines, and in Britain from the *Motoring Which?* road-test reports, which are extremely helpful. Remember that if you're disposing of an existing car, it's worth running through this check-list in relation to that as well, to remind yourself of exactly what you thought was good or bad about it — this will help to concentrate your thoughts in relation to your new machine.

CHECK-LIST

★ **Space** — too obvious to need much elaboration. If you or any of your likely passengers are long in the leg, can you occupy the car comfortably without supporting your chin with your knees? How much adjustment is there in the seating, and possibly in the steering-wheel position? If you have children you need to shoehorn protestingly in and out of baby-seats, would there be a virtue in looking for a four-door model rather than a two-door? Is there enough headroom? How about the luggage space? And can you store maps, guidebooks and any other useful paperwork somewhere sensible where it isn't constantly spilling on to the floor?

★ **Handling, performance and reliability** — what is its standing-start and low-speed acceleration like? Will it attain a motorway cruising speed (60-70 mph) and keep it without undue engine or transmission noise which can be tiring on a long journey? Can you park it easily? Are its pedals positioned sensibly, or are they awkward to operate? (Some designs set the accelerator pedal much further forward than the other pedals, so that in an emergency quite a substantial split-second is taken up in moving from the throttle to the brake.) Are its brakes light to operate but effective, its hand-brake capable of holding the car on a steep incline? Is the visibility good, at front and rear? Does it roll uncomfortably on corners, or pitch from end to end on sharp acceleration or braking?

★ **Running costs** — what does the road-test report reveal about its petrol consumption? Is it expensive to insure? How expensive will spare parts be, and how easy to obtain? How near to your home is the relevant agency for the car?

Now work out a budget. Start with the figure you think you can reasonably afford for the car. Add on the road tax, which at time of writing is £100 per year, and the annual cost of insurance — for which you should obtain two or three competing quotes either from brokers or direct from the insurance companies. If you're using the car for work, this will inflate the cost of insurance quite considerably, though it depends on what your work is. If you're buying a new car, take account of depreciation — around 30% in the first year, 15% in the second and 10% a year thereafter. Discover from the agents the cost of a standard service, the kind they would expect to do every 5,000 miles or so, which you'd be likely to need at least once a year and very likely more often, depending on your mileage.

BUYING NEW

If you're buying a new car, start with the manufacturer's brochures and the *Motoring Which?* reports. Whilst exploring the specifications and performance figures, think also about your own performance — financially.

To start with, if you have the cash, pay the cash. A bank loan or a finance-house deal will inevitably cost you more in interest than you would gain from investing the money, unless you're psychic about stocks and shares or the 3.30 at Newmarket. If the bank lends you the money, you'll be able to work out the rate of repayment and the period of repayment in a manner — to some extent — to suit yourself. If a finance house is the lender, and this is an arrangement usually set up through the garage from which you're buying the car, the deal will generally be that a third of the price is to be paid on agreement, and the remainder over a period of two years.

HP is often more convenient, because if you've suddenly fallen in love with the car of your dreams your first thought will be to get it into your clutches at the earliest opportunity. It isn't the cheapest however, because there are more links in the chain. The finance house is itself borrowing from a bank, and the dealer will be getting a cut for introducing you to the delights of indebtedness.

The Consumer Credit Act has helped to make this territory much less of a minefield for the unwary, though you still have to watch your step, and not everybody in either the motor trade or the loan business is an obvious candidate for sitting on the right hand of God, which will come as no surprise. The Act has, however, meant that you can change your mind, as long as you don't dawdle too long over it. You now have five days to opt out after you receive the copy of the agreement at home. And if you get behind with payments, it isn't as easy as it used to be for the company to repossess the car.

Your creditworthiness will be checked out through the credit data agencies, and if you sport a list of fraud convictions the finance house may politely raise objections about the deal. If they turn you down, you do have the right to find out why, to have access to a copy of the file that blew the whistle on you, and to get it altered if you can prove the record is in error.

Then you have to stump up the one-third down payment. Your old car in part-exchange may suffice for this. If you're able to pay the whole sum in readies, then you may be able to persuade the dealer to offer you a discount for cash — maybe 10%. At slack times of the car trading year — immediately before Christmas and through to the New Year, and in July when dealers are getting rid of old stock before the new registration letter is introduced — you may be able to get better deals out of garages.

If you're self-employed or running a business for which the car will be used, you may want to explore the tax advantages of **leasing**, a system whereby the finance company buys the car and leases it to you for two or three years. At the end of the lease you can either buy it for the percentage of its original price you agreed at the outset, or let the company have it back and pay the difference between the original figure and what the car actually makes on the market.

INSURANCE

The law obliges you to have **third-party** insurance before you take a car out on the road. This means that if you hit something or someone, or you injure a passenger in your own vehicle, the cost of repairs and compensation will be borne by an insurance company. **Comprehensive** insurance is a more expensive variant, intended to cover the cost of repairs to your own car when not the responsibility of some other offending party. It also covers injury to other people and property, includes some cover for yourself and covers fire or accidental damage to your vehicle, theft of the car itself and to some extent its contents. Generally, people who drive old bangers opt for third-party insurance on the grounds that the repair costs on serious damage might exceed the value of the car. Where this isn't the case, missing out on comprehensive insurance can turn out to be a false economy if you ever have a serious prang.

Insurance brokers, to be found in nearly every high street, or in the classified directories, will do all the chasing around to get competing quotes from different insurance companies, and they often have the experience and expertise to be able to solve problem cases — such as customers who have a poor driving record, or drivers of very exotic sports cars, or the very young or old, all of whom might have difficulty in obtaining insurance.

Some points worth checking with the broker are the availability of an instalment plan for paying the premium, whether there is any provision for the cost of hiring a car if yours is off the road, whether the company will pay for a new replacement if a brand-new car is written off, and whether windscreen insurance is offered separately so that a claim on it doesn't affect your no-claims bonus.

The **no-claims bonus** is an important feature of the economics of motor insurance. Most companies reduce the premium by 30% if you don't make a claim against them in the first year, 40% for two years and so on, rising to 60%, after which the reduction tails off. This kind of provision makes cheaper repairs worth forking out for yourself, though you may in any case already have received a discount for agreeing to contribute an initial sum to any repair bill. This is called an **excess**.

The insurance broker will tell you which **insurance grouping** your car — or would-be car — falls into. If you're doing your homework prior to purchase, this news may well affect your decision to buy one model rather than another, and on the face of it the decision governing the car's classification may not follow any apparent logic at all.

There are eight insurance categories in Britain, ranging from the cheapest in Group 1 to the most expensive in Group 8. At the extreme ends, the classifications tend to make sense — with the most basic and widely available family saloons at one end, and very specialized imported cars, for which repair costs might be astronomical, at the other. Cars at the top end might cost three times as much to insure as those at the bottom, so checking out this aspect of your purchase beforehand makes a lot of sense. Factors that govern the classification — apart from obvious ones such as sportiness and high performance, which the insurers might regard as an invitation to recklessness — will be the repair costs and availability and cost of spares. Continental cars tend to be put in higher groupings for this reason, though some foreign manufacturers have realized that this is a disincentive to purchase and so offer special insurance deals of their own, arranged through the dealer. If you have to switch from another insurer, however, you'll lose the no-claims discount.

Where you live will make a difference to insurance costs, and so will your work or personal circumstances. Students have problems obtaining cheap insurance — so do journalists, unfortunately.

PROTECTION

The Supply of Goods Act and dealing with a member of either the Motor Agents' Association or the Scottish Motor Trade Association give you some leverage in Britain. The former obliges professional retailers to sell items of 'merchantable quality' i.e. items that are able to do what the retailer has stated they can do, and that fit the purpose they were built for. This legislation has created conditions such that nowadays most dealers with the manufacturer's franchise will not argue about repairs under guarantee. And most new-car guarantees last for a year, though some manufacturers these days are getting either so confident in their products or so enthusiastic to compete that they are starting to offer longer guarantee periods. You pay for this extra service in the purchase price, just the same.

Technically, the Act also applies to used vehicles — or used anything — but actually getting compensation is a tougher job. Used cars, unless guaranteed on specific components by the dealer, tend to be sold 'as seen' and therefore if there is a defect that ought to have been obvious to you when you bought it, you'll have a hard time crying 'foul' later on.

With **new cars** the after-sale protection tends to be quite comprehensive, though it may be subject to certain stipulations. The manufacturer will certainly specify as a condition of the guarantee that the car is serviced only by an agency it approves of, that approved spares are used and that the car is not modified in ways unauthorized by the makers. The guarantee will also certainly prohibit the owner from hiring out the car or using it for competitions. The provisions of the guarantee are increasingly being extended to recovery deals in the event of breakdowns, and to reimbursement for car-hire charges and other inconveniences.

All this is naturally far more restricted in the case of **used cars**, though deals applying to them are improving. Warranty systems are now available, with the cost built into the purchase price. These cover repairs for periods from three months to a year, though the same stipulations about where you get the car serviced may apply as do with new cars. Such warranties may also cover only major components — such as the engine, the gearbox and the final drive. Some warranties only cover the cost of parts, and with current labour prices the final bill will be very much higher.

PRIVATE SALES

If you buy a car privately, most of the legislation doesn't help you. You can, in theory, take someone to court if they have sold you a car under a smokescreen of the most awful baloney, but it's expensive, tedious and if you lose you wind up with not only a lousy motor car but legal costs as well. Some canny folk run used-car businesses from their own homes and thus side-step most of the legal obligations, and if you locate a car through a magazine or the local paper, you may well find the same phone number or address appearing repeatedly.

That there is very little compensation available to the buyer when the purchase expires before they've even got it home is not entirely a form of Sod's Law. The vendor may well have parted with the car in perfectly good faith, and if they don't know much about cars themselves — or even if they do — may have been genuinely unaware that a valve was just about to drop through a piston, or the automatic gearbox lock solid. The onus is on the purchaser to make a proper check and then look elsewhere if the car seems delectable on the surface but treacherous under the skin. Which is why the following section is particularly weighted towards proper scrutiny of the bits and pieces, as well as being simply a run-down on how to understand the specifications that manufacturers sell their new cars on. Both areas are well worth some careful study.

BUYING — THE VIRTUES OF DOING YOUR HOMEWORK

When you're trying to fathom out what on earth the specifications in the manufacturers' glossy brochures actually mean, it's well worth the effort to obtain the Consumers' Association's *Motoring Which?*, which is written in a manner designed to be user-friendly for car-buyers.

By now, if you've made any sense of the previous chapter, you should know what the sales pitch is talking about when it quotes the number of cylinders in the engine, the bore (the diameter of the pistons) and the stroke (the distance they travel down the cylinder), the type of valve gear, fuel system and so on. There will then probably be figures for the **brake horsepower (bhp)** and the **torque** of the engine.

The manufacturer has obtained the first figure by testing the engine on the bench, and using it to drive a **brake**, which for our purposes is simply a device that introduces a load that the engine has to push against. It's a measure of the force exerted by the pistons against a load, and it will be expressed as **gross bhp** or **net bhp**, and also at a given engine speed, generally between 4,500 and 5,500 revolutions per minute (rpm). The net figure is more useful, because it takes into account how much clout the engine has left after it has performed such functions as driving the dynamo and the fan, and the figure may range from 20 bhp for a very small car to 120 or so for a high-performance one.

Torque is a measure of leverage, i.e. how good the car will be at getting you up that hill with the family and the luggage or the bulkiest refugees from the office party on board, and in this respect it's a much more useful measurement than bhp. If you think about it, what matters in leverage is the length of the lever and how red in the face you're going trying to do some useful work with it. Translated to the internal combustion engine, this means the length of travel of the piston down the cylinder and the amount of force applied to it by the expanding gas on the ignition stroke.

From the point of view of understanding the spec, a good rule of thumb is that if the maximum torque figure occurs at 3,500 rpm or so, then you'll be likely to have to use the gears quite busily to keep the car pulling on hills. If the peak figure occurs at, say, 500 to 1000 rpm lower, then the car is likely to be good on hills and this will also improve the fuel economy.

If you're going to compare acceleration times, don't simply do it from standing starts, but also check what kind of acceleration the manufacturer quotes as available in top gear at cruising speeds — say between 30 mph and 50 mph. Fuel-consumption figures can also be taken with a pinch of salt, and the figures in independent reports are likely to be more useful. What kind of driver you are, and where you mostly drive the car, will also affect the fuel-consumption figures quite substantially.

CULTIVATING THE EAGLE EYE

On **new cars**, you shouldn't need to do a particularly obsessive check, though it's usually more convenient to get minor faults corrected before you take possession rather than afterwards. In the course of being delivered from one part of the country to another, new cars do sometimes develop faults and blemishes and it's worth having a good look at the bodywork and making a note of any of these. Check the lights as well, the panel warning lamps and all the ancillaries such as window de-misters, washers, wipers, heaters and window winders, and make sure that all the doors (including the boot) close easily and lock as they should. You're legally entitled to be furnished with a copy of the manufacturer's pre-delivery check-list, and you should go through this with the car yourself and make sure that the dealer puts any defects right.

But it's buying **second hand**, with all the lack of protection for the purchaser we've described above, that requires some really close attention. If you're not willing to do the homework, then take someone along with you who knows something about cars, and be prepared to abandon a prospective purchase if the vendor makes a fuss about the length of time you spend looking it over.

You can buy from a dealer, or at an auction, or privately through small ads in local newspapers. If a dealer is selling the car, carefully check the terms of any guarantee being offered, ascertain whether it's for parts or labour or both, and get any repairs that the dealer agrees to do before you take possession itemized on paper. Remember that the Supply of Goods Act as it applies to motor cars requires that a motor car sold in going order has got to be road-worthy in order to be able to perform the function it's intended for. So if your purchase turns out not to be, you may have some leverage through the legislation. Auctions are altogether a more dicey proposition unless you really know what you're doing. Some good deals turn up in auctions, but a lot of dumping of undesirables goes on there too, and you don't get the opportunity to do a road test before purchase.

In more normal circumstances of second-hand buying, the motoring organizations will provide a service pretty much like the one a surveyor provides when you buy a house — but you have to pay for it, and you can't usually secure it immediately, which may be a problem if there are several people in the running for the car. Garages will sometimes do the same thing, though possibly in a less systematic way.

The **price** for which the car is on offer can be checked against the going price quoted in a publication such as the *Motorists' Guide to New and Used Car Prices*. For any given year of manufacture, the prices will still be variable, because the **mileage** is a major consideration, as well as the general condition. The mileage is recorded on a little window in the centre of the speedometer. Generally, the further above 20,000 miles a car has travelled, the more the risk of breakdowns increases, but on a well-maintained car completely unexpected failures shouldn't happen and the more expensive faults will announce their presence in the form of noise or odd behaviour for a while before anything terminal occurs. As is now well known, mileage readings can be altered by sharp-fingered individuals, so the reading shouldn't be taken as gospel. Comparison of the current mileage figure with figures entered on previous MOT certificates and service-station invoices is one guide to accuracy, as is comparison of the figure with the general condition of the car.

The vendor may be able to produce invoices for major replacements, which can sometimes be balanced against the car's mileage. But these should determine your decision either to buy or to look elsewhere rather than making a vast difference to the price. Evidence of engine or gearbox replacement is useful to the next owner, but not to the extent that the vendor can jack the price up substantially.

Beware of re-sprays on second-hand cars, particularly an all-over re-spray. It may well have been done simply because the owner fancied driving a car in pink with blue spots, but it's much more likely to have been done to conceal rust or accident damage. However nice the job seems to be, it's as well to be very suspicious. Many under-the-railway-arches refurbishments of tatty or crash-damaged cars don't keep their chirpy glossiness much beyond the first spell of wet weather, and the tell-tale blisters of rust burrowing away under the paintwork eventually start appearing with the frequency of adolescent spots.

One last warning on second-hand buying before we get down to the serious business of checking over the goods. You need to be as sure as you can be that the person selling you the car has a right to sell it, and that your exotic purchase isn't suddenly going to be repossessed by the constabulary while you're breezing around the highways trying to impress a friend. Checking out previous owners named on the registration document is a help. It's also more likely to be a respectable deal if you're buying the car at the vendor's home and not in an underground car-park in the middle of the night from somebody wearing a false beard. You can't be lumbered by finance companies in Britain for unknowingly buying a car that still has unpaid instalments on it, but you can be obliged to relinquish a stolen car, and, if you bought it privately, getting the compensation might turn out to be the kind of job for which you'll need a squad of private detectives.

GETTING UP CLOSE

A few simple implements to commence the examination: take with you a medium-sized screwdriver, a magnet, some tissues and a flashlight. Even with such modest preparations, you're all set to take on the worst the used-car jungle can throw at you. Remember, anyone can get stung buying a used car, even an expert. The major fault that only betrays itself after you've signed on the dotted line is a perpetual nightmare, but with a little preparation you can minimize the risks. It's also advisable to go over all these points beforehand on a car belonging to someone you know, so that you get fairly brisk at carrying it all out. This will minimize the likelihood of your rushing the check when you come to do it 'live' because you think your fumbling efforts are inducing the vendor to view you with that 'what a wally' look. Try to read some road tests for the model you're interested in, and maybe have a chat with someone who has owned one — both of these enquiries may bring to light weak points on the vehicle which you will then be forewarned about when you come to look at one.

Taking a friend with you is always a good idea in such circumstances, ideally someone who knows a bit about motor cars, better still someone who knows the model in question. One, if you're female it unfortunately makes sense to do this when visiting total strangers in obscure parts of town, and two, whatever gender you are, a second person can help pass the time with the vendor and not make you feel you have to dash through everything.

Start by warning the vendor that you're expecting to spend some time looking at the car — possibly 30 minutes to an hour — and that you want to conduct a fairly extensive examination. If the car's owner is unhappy about this, say bye-bye.

Assuming you're still in the running, first check the mileage reading on the speedometer. At a mileage below 30,000, the car is likely to be clean, free of serious rust, possibly scruffy inside but not shabby and — as long as there is some written evidence of regular maintenance — likely to provide good service from its major components for some time. If a car of this mileage nevertheless does seem surprisingly battered about, it may be an indication of very hard use without much care for the car, or of an untrue mileage reading. The latter suspicion may be backed up by, for instance, severe wear on the upholstery and carpets that implies more use than the reading suggests, or a lot of wear on the rubber pedal pads.

Between 30,000 and 50,000 miles there is much more likelihood of a need for major replacements, particularly of the clutch and brake parts. Upwards of 50,000, anything could happen, and you do need to be on your guard about the condition of the main components — the engine, gearbox and final drive. At this mileage the owner may, however, be able to furnish you with bills for replacement or reconditioned engines and transmissions, in which case, if the rest of the car is sound, you may be on to a bargain. Whilst on the subject of paperwork, take a look at the registration document and the MOT certificate before you go any further. The former will indicate if the car has ever been a reclaimed write-off, and the latter should in any case be available, and current. If there is a problem with either of these, head for your next appointment.

You should always try to look at your prospective purchase in a good light, and by that we don't mean in a spirit of jovial optimism. It's not a good idea to buy cars at night, or by the light of street-lamps. Look along the sides of the car to see if there are ripples in the bodywork — if the paint job has been quite professional, the gloss may hide damaged bodywork on a cursory glance, but a squint from end to end of the car tends to show it up. Crouching at the front and then at the back, make sure that the car sits level on the ground. If it doesn't, there may be a fault in the suspension, or worse still the bodywork may have been knocked out of line in a crash.

Check the fit of the doors and the boot, and the effectiveness of the locks. Once again, if the car has been in a shunt, the fit of these items tends to be affected, unless repairs have been done thoroughly. Remember that if the doors don't shut well, the reason may also be the much less formidable one that the hinges are worn, which you'll be able to tell if you can rock the open door up and down. Replacing the hinges is not an expensive matter, but if the car is sufficiently long in the tooth for the hinges to be gone, then it's sufficiently long in the tooth for many other things to be on the way out as well.

Now look closely at the rubber seals around the windows, bonnet, boot, and lamps. We cautioned earlier on against buying fully resprayed cars unless you're absolutely certain that the respray was only cosmetic and not designed to conceal rust or damage. One way of rumbling a quick back-street respray is to look for signs of overspray of the new paint on the rubber seals, since bodgy sprayers usually can't be bothered to remove all these bits before painting, or their masking techniques are sloppy.

Rust is your biggest enemy. Faulty mechanical components you can replace — at a price — but severe rust damage on a 'metal-box' or monocoque car can lead to a series of very dispiriting journeys in and out of MOT testing stations and it reduces the resale value more quickly than anything. The most vulnerable spots on any car, logically enough, are the places where moist road dirt thrown up by the wheels gets lodged and starts corroding the panels from the inside. This may happen around the headlamps, behind the front wheels where the inner wing joins the rest of the body, in the box sections running along under the doors, and just in front of the rear wheels where the inner rear wing joins the main bodywork.

Rust may have occurred in these places and been bodged to camouflage it. The most frequently used quick-repair material is **fibreglass resin**, a reinforced plastic which can be applied to a rust-hole or a damaged area when wet and then sets rock hard so that it can be sanded and painted — and a well-executed job with this stuff can be very hard to detect by eye alone. This is where you produce, with a flourish, your **magnet**, the most sophisticated tool you need for discovering this. Pass the magnet over the sound bits of metalwork and it will stick, but when you get to the dodgy areas it won't, and you'll know that fibreglass has been used there — which can be confirmed by touch, because fibreglassed areas are usually thicker than the original metalwork.

It's normally difficult or inconvenient to get **underneath** a car when it's parked in front of someone's house and it's pouring with rain or the local dogs have left evidence of their presence around the car, but if you can see at least a little way underneath it's a big help. (**But remember: don't either attempt yourself, or accept the vendor's invitation, to go underneath the car while it's supported on a jack. Crawling under supported cars calls for proper use of axle stands or ramps as well as a jack, and some people who have ignored this advice are no longer with us.**)

If you can get a view of the suspension gear and the brakes by the unedifying process of lying in the road with a flashlight (make sure you're not lying in a street in the face of oncoming traffic), look for any signs of rust under the floor and on any bits of the metal brake pipes that you can see. If it's an old car and you find that the underside is sporting a spanking new coating of underseal, which is a black nobbly bitumen paint, then be very suspicious. People don't usually underseal old vehicles that weren't undersealed when new unless they're covering up all manner of bodges and patches underneath.

If you do see areas that look slightly rusty, give them a poke with a screwdriver, and if the vendor looks shocked, simply say that this is only what happens to the car in an MOT testing station anyway. Sometimes horrifically large holes magically appear on surfaces that at first looked merely a bit shabby, or marred with the odd pin-hole. Also prod around the points where the wheels and springs are mounted to the bodywork, and around the jacking points — which may be apertures let into the bottom of the box sections running under the doors, or simply strengthened sections just ahead of the rear wheels and just behind the front ones. If you are in doubt about their condition, get the jack out and use it to lift the car at these points. If they're seriously rusty you may find that the jack goes on going up and the car stays firmly on the ground, to the accompaniment of loud tearing sounds — representing either ripping metal or the vendor's hair being voluntarily removed, or both.

While you're down there, take a look at the silencer for any signs of extensive rusting (steel silencers don't have an enormously long life anyway, but a collapsing one may be an argument for a reduction in the price) and also for any evidence of oil or water leaks. Locate the drive shafts, which (if you remember your apprenticeship in Chapter Two) transmit the drive from the differential to the wheels. To avoid looking too much of a nerd to the vendor, you should already know whether the car is a front- or a rear-wheel drive before you ever get to this stage. Grip each drive shaft underneath the car and try to twist them. They should barely move at all. If there is any appreciable slack, it indicates wear in the joints at either end of the shaft.

Last of all while you're on your hands and knees, take a look at the tyres. Run your fingers over the tyre walls, on the surfaces facing into the car as well as the outside, and see if you can detect any suspicious bulges or splits. The tread depth, which is the depth of the little valleys between the corrugations on the running surface of the tyre, should be at least 1 mm to prevent unwelcome accusations from the police. If you discover that the front tyres have been unevenly worn — so that the tread depth is good on the outside of the tyre but poor on the inside — that's a sign that the steering gear is out of true. This may require no more than a simple adjustment by a service station, but it may also be a sign that the steering has been knocked askew in a smash, and you should then press the vendor on this point, and look carefully for further evidence.

Now you open the bonnet. Cleanliness in the engine compartment isn't everything — because the dodgier motor traders these days are only too aware of how cost-effective a bit of judicious valeting inside and out can be — but a clean engine can be a good sign of careful maintenance and some affectionate interest in the well-being of the machine. Look at the plug leads and the distributor cap — these should be clean and free from grease. If they're covered in grime, that means neglected servicing, and may also account for any erratic behaviour in the performance of the car.

Take one of the tissues from your hi-tech tool-kit, locate the oil dip-stick, which will be sticking up vertically on one or other side of the engine block, remove it, wipe it clean, reinsert it until it won't go in any further, then withdraw it again and check the oil level against the manufacturer's marking on the stick. If it's very low, that's a sign of poor maintenance, and possibly indicates that the engine is burning oil. You'll be able to discover more evidence of oil incineration when you drive the car. If there are bubbles of water in the oil on the stick, this may indicate that water is leaking from the cooling system into the oil — again, not good news, and possibly a symptom of gasket leaks or cracks. Taking the oil filler cap off the valve cover on the top of the engine and peering in there to see if there is any froth and muck is also a useful way of checking for signs of neglect or of water getting where it shouldn't.

If you haven't already jacked up the car, jack up each front wheel in turn now. Once the wheel is free of the ground, grasp it with both hands at the top of the tyre and attempt to rock it vertically. **Once again, don't get into a position where any part of you could be trapped if the jack failed**. There should be no movement in the wheel, and if there is, it means there's play (a cheerful-sounding engineer's term for wear) in the steering swivels or the wheel bearings — which would lead to an instant MOT failure. Perform this test on each front wheel, then let the car back on to the ground. Sticking your arm through the driver's door window, rock the steering wheel from side to side and watch for the movement at the roadwheel — the latter should respond to the steering-wheel movement at once. If there's a delay before anything happens, then there may be wear in the steering gear. Your assistant can confirm whether there is a similar delay at the roadwheel on the other side of the car.

Before you get in and attempt to take to the roads, push down each wing in turn against the suspension pressure and then let it go. The car should immediately settle back into a stable position. If it bounces a bit before it stops, this is an indication of wear in the shock-absorbers.

DRIVING

As in any strange car, check the whereabouts of all the driving instruments, including the direction indicators and the horn, and adjust the position of the rear-view mirror. Then turn on the ignition. Warning lights should illuminate for the oil pressure and the generator circuit. On modern cars, these will usually be represented by a symbol — a line drawing of a battery for the generator circuit, and a picture of an oil can for the oil pressure.

Start the engine. It should start without undue protest, too much turning over of the engine on the starter, or lots of coughs, wheezes and false starts before it fires. Rev up the engine and both the warning lights that came on with the ignition should go out and stay out.

If the car has a manual gearbox, gently explore the feel of the clutch pedal with your foot. There should be an inch or so of movement as you depress it before you start to feel the resistance of the springs inside the clutch. If the clutch feels stiff right from the start, it may simply be because of an unlubricated clutch operating cable, but it may be a sign of wear in the clutch itself, which will be further revealed as you drive the car.

Put the car in gear, and gently bring the clutch up to move off, but initially with the handbrake still on. The car should stall. If it moves off smoothly, it means that your handbrake is out of adjustment or the rear brakes are worn. If the engine speed rises without the car doing anything, it's a sign of clutch wear — because, if you recall our 'naming of parts' exercise in the previous chapter, the clutch is a sandwich of plates. If these plates are worn, they may not form a firm sandwich and will continue to slip even when the clutch is fully engaged, which will prevent the power from properly getting to the wheels. Now release the handbrake and move off normally. This should occur smoothly and without judders or noise. Juddery take-up is similarly a sign of clutch decline.

In the early stages of the test don't start rushing about until you've had an opportunity to test progressively the effectiveness of the brakes. They should retard the car smoothly but positively, without undue noise (brake squeak can be a characteristic of some cars, particularly in wet weather, but there should be no metallic noises or graunching sounds) and without causing the car to swerve to one side or the other. If the brakes seem unsafe to you, don't drive the car any further.

Whilst driving, check the condition of all the gear ratios — there should be no knocking sounds or whining in any of them, and no jumping out of gear either. Check the engine's acceleration and its freedom from undue mechanical noises or knockings either when accelerating or when the car goes on to the 'overrun' — which is what happens when you lift your foot off the accelerator for the vehicle to run downhill. As you do this, you may hear a clunk from somewhere in the transmission immediately you cease acceleration and let the car roll. If you do, it indicates wear in the drive shafts or the differential. Whilst driving at around 30 mph in third gear, jab your foot on and off the accelerator a few times — the car will begin to snatch, but there shouldn't be any clunks or mechanical noises. If there are, it's a further sign of transmission wear.

If the model you're looking at sports front-wheel drive, find a suitable open space, such as a car-park, and drive the car slowly round in a tight circle. If there is wear in the 'constant velocity' joints through which the drive is transmitted from the differential to the steered wheels, you will hear it as a constant clicking and clacking from the front wheels.

Run the car on a clear straight road without too steep a camber — if you can find one — and momentarily take your hands off the steering wheel to check if the car begins to slew to one side. Provided that the road isn't wet or greasy, check for the same tendency in the brakes by performing an emergency stop, **once you're sure that there are no hazards in front of you or behind you**. The car should pull up quickly and without swerving.

Return to the vendor's premises. Get out of the car and get your trusty assistant, or the owner, to rev up the engine briskly while you watch the exhaust. Clouds of greyish-blue smoke are a sure sign of wear in the valves or pistons and an indication that you should leave the car alone. Pungent black smoke indicates an over-rich fuel mixture.

Lastly check the operation of all the ancillaries: the horn, the wipers, all the lights (including the brake lights) and the indicators.

5

LOOKING AFTER IT

'When he has nothing special
on hand he stretches himself out under his motor car and
contemplates it piece by piece,
bolt by bolt, screw by screw, in long,
strange colloquy with his machine.'
(*Luigi Barzini*, Peking to Paris)

So far so good. You've bought the car of your dreams and are keeping your fingers crossed that it won't turn out to be the transport of your nightmares. If you've roughly familiarized yourself with the way cars work and taken care with the purchase as suggested in the last chapter, the latter shouldn't turn out to be the case unless the fates are really against you — and even if they are, we have some anti-fates training to come in a later chapter.

So now it's sitting smugly in your garage or outside your front door, and you're smugly staring at it. How your relationship develops will depend on how much of a bastard or a saint it turns out to be, but also on how much rudimentary preparation you put into smoothing the way.

The first thing you should have to hand is the **owner's handbook**. The manufacturers say you should read this before doing very much else, and although the owner's handbook is of limited use, they're right just the same. If the original one for the car has been lost, write to the manufacturers to obtain one, or get one through the local agent.

The virtue of the handbook is that the information and the way it's presented tends to be aimed at the driver who may be pretty inexperienced with motor cars — it tells you where everything on your particular car actually is, it simply describes what you need to know to make it work, and it also outlines rudimentary maintenance procedures that every owner-driver should be familiar with. Usually the illustrations are clear, and you'll feel much more at home with your purchase once you've taken stock of it.

Now consider the virtues of joining one of the **motoring organizations** functioning in your particular part of the world. You really need to belong to a national one, and preferably one that also offers some assistance when you're driving abroad — it's a considerable comfort to know that for a fairly modest annual outlay you can quickly summon assistance to a roadside breakdown, and also get the car trailered to wherever you're going if something goes wrong that can't be fixed on the spot. You may ask, why bother to find out anything else about the car or carry any tools or spares, if you can call up an expert to do it all for you anyway? The answer is, usually, time. Malevolent fates decree that breakdowns rarely happen close to a working telephone, that they frequently happen in bad weather or during busy traffic periods when the services are already stretched, and that they are also fond of occurring in picturesque out-of-the-way spots so that it can take cavalry quite a long time to get to the scene. If it is something simple that can be fixed, with a bit of cursing and grimy fingernails, in half an hour or so, it's useful to know how.

Thirdly, you should work out who's going to **service** the car for you. If you bought it under a guarantee, you may have no choice in this, because the terms of the warranty may specify a particular agent. If this isn't the case, then for obvious reasons it's useful to find an establishment close to either your home or your workplace. The best recommendations are got by word of mouth and you should ask motoring friends for any suggestions.

Of course, very tatty back-street one-person operations do occasionally reveal mechanical geniuses who are also as honest as the day they were born, and the poshness of a garage's premises is not necessarily any indication of its reliability. However, bigger garages have a reputation to protect, and may belong to a traders' association that has a code of practice to be observed, and if they have a franchise to represent the manufacturer of your particular car, then you can complain to said manufacturer if you're dissatisfied. Back-street operations can certainly be cheaper and are often skilful but it helps if they've been strongly recommended by someone you trust.

You should already have ascertained during the pre-purchase once-over whether essential tools such as the car's jack and jack-handle and its wheelbrace are present and in working order. If they aren't, but the car otherwise came up to scratch, these are items you should immediately purchase because there's nothing more exasperating than having a puncture that you proudly possess the know-how to fix but not the equipment. Also check the tools that come with the car, if there are any. Tools supplied as standard on new cars are very rudimentary compared with what they used to be like, and a succession of owners of a used car may well have walked off with what tools there were anyway.

GOING SHOPPING

Start by making a shopping list of items you need from the local car-accessory emporium. This may seem like quite a tall order when you've just lobbed out a fortune to buy the car in the first place, but it will certainly make its money back quite quickly. In fact if you have to call a garage out for a roadside repair you know you could have done yourself, or wait for one of the motoring organizations to come out to you while you miss a crucial business meeting, you could find yourself saying goodbye to the equivalent of the bill for this shopping expedition in the space of just one mishap.

The following will repay being carried on the car at all times:

- **Jack and wheelbrace**. These should be the ones that came with the car when it was new. If it's a used car and they're missing, buy a standard jack and a 'spider' type wheelbrace — that's a wheelbrace that looks like a cross, with four alternative wheel-nut sizes on it. Tell the accessory shop what car it is, because not all cars use metric nut sizes, particularly not older ones. The jacks you're likely to be offered are either **scissors-jacks**, which you raise by turning a long screw with a lever, or **hydraulic bottle-jacks**. The latter are more expensive, but much less hard work to use, since you have to exert only very gentle pressure on a lever to get them to lift the car.

- **Tyre pump with pressure gauge**. This is a foot-pump with a dial-gauge attached so that you can read off the pressure of the tyres. Garage forecourts do have air-lines and pressure gauges, of course, but they're quite often badly maintained, inaccurate or not functioning at all, and tyre pumps are not expensive.

TOOLS

Only real enthusiasts, or experts who have absolutely no faith in the reliability of their cars, carry back-breaking loads of tools around in the boot. But it makes sense to carry a small tool-roll or tool-box containing the following:

- **Set of open-ended spanners**. Again, tell the accessory shop what your car is, because the age and type of car and the part of the world it was built in will determine what specifications of nuts and bolts it has — the owner's handbook should provide the same information. Buy the best spanners you can afford, because cheaper ones that have not been effectively hardened will slip on the nuts, causing damage to your car, your fingers and your brain. If you're feeling flush, invest in a set of **ring spanners** of the same specification to go alongside the open-ended ones. Ring spanners completely surround the nut, and although they can't always be used in tight corners, they are a much more reliable means of extracting nuts and bolts without damaging them. And if you want to get really flash, or you don't mind being given the kind of Christmas or birthday present that people in woolly jerseys are depicted gloating over in mail-order catalogues, you could even go as far as a **socket set**. This is a set of a very sophisticated type of spanners, with steel sockets that fit over the nuts, which can be manipulated by a variety of different levers and joints to fit into the most awkward spaces. Once again, do make sure *what sort of nut type* your car has. If you get the wrong sort, some of the sockets may still fit, but they won't fit well and you'll quickly be driven mad by the sockets slipping and rounding the edges of the nuts and bolts to the point where no spanner on earth will be able to extract them. Make sure also that you get hold of the right-sized spanner to remove the **sump drain plug**, which is the means by which old oil can be drained out of the engine. A ring spanner, or preferably a socket, is essential for the drain plug. Some cars use their own particular variant of plug wrench for this component, so if it isn't a normal bolt head find out from the handbook or the local agents what kind of wrench you need.

- **Screwdrivers**. Three would make sense — a very small one for electrical fittings, a medium-sized plain one and a medium cross-headed Philips type.

- **A plug spanner**. This is a special cylindrical spanner that fits snugly over the sparking plugs and can reach into the recessed holes in the cylinder head where the plugs sit. Some of the better ones have a rubber insert that grips the plug and helps you draw it out.

- **A mole wrench**. This is a kind of adjustable spanner, but one that exerts a fearsome grip on the object it's removing. It's not intended for use where a regular spanner would fit instead, because it always leaves its teeth-marks on anything it touches, but it's an invaluable fall-back when nothing else will do.

- **Pliers**. Buy a fairly robust-looking pair, preferably including a wire-cutter.

- **Battery jump-leads**. These are very thick electric cables with clamps on the ends. You use them to link a knight in shining-armour's battery to your own when yours is flat and the car won't start. Again, buy the best ones you can. Some cheap ones are very thin, and provide more fizzing noises and smoke than practical assistance when it comes to trying to start the machine.

- **Flashlight**. Get a big robust one, not just a domestic torch. If you get the type that also has a flashing emergency mode, you can use it to warn oncoming or following traffic in a breakdown or an accident.

- **Roll of insulating tape**. Accessory shops often stock a pack that includes both electrical insulating tape and a heat-resistant tape that can be used to bind up leaking water-hoses. If you can get both, do so.

- **Silencer bandage**. This is an unpleasant-looking brown tape that becomes pliable when damp. If your exhaust blows a leak, you can bind this stuff round it according to the instructions on the package and it hardens under the heat of the engine to act as an effective temporary repair.

- **Set of feeler gauges**. This is a collection of thin strips of metal, the purpose of which we'll go into in more detail as we press on. Suffice to say that these strips of metal are all of different thicknesses, and measure the critical gaps in such components as sparking plugs and contact points. Make sure you discover whether you need a metric or an imperial set for your particular car.

There are a few items that you can include in this shopping spree that won't be kept on the car but are very handy to have around. One that you wouldn't ordinarily travel with, but should keep at home in some place where you don't have to ransack the house to find it, is a **battery-charger**. This is simply a kind of transformer that takes the electrical supply from the house mains and converts it into a suitable output for the car battery, which it then brings back to its full capacity. Stored near your battery-charger you ought to keep a bottle of **distilled water** for topping up the battery fluid — accessory shops will sell it with a special dispenser on top for controlling the flow. Also buy, as an inevitable necessity in the future, some **touch-up paint** for those scrapes and blemishes that always turn up from time to time. You can't just go for something that looks roughly like your paintwork, because there are thousands of car colours, and they all differ by fine variations of shade that nevertheless stick out like a sore thumb if you apply the wrong one. The name and serial number of the paint will be located on a plaque somewhere on the car (the handbook will say where), and if you can't find it the local agent for the make will tell you what the colour is, and will probably be able to supply the touch-up paint as well. It's useful to have both an aerosol of the correct colour, and a small brush applicator for very limited areas.

Keep to hand also a small quantity of **rust-killer**, of which there are many kinds on the market. They all work by chemical action, converting the rust into an inert compound, but it's labour-saving to use one that acts as a primer for the new paint as well.

It's also sensible to keep at home a mixture of ordinary tap-water and **antifreeze**, mixed in the proportions recommended by the maker of the latter. (If you're in touch with the maker of the former, then probably most of the advice contained in this book will be redundant.) This is for topping up the radiator when necessary.

SPARE PARTS

You should also carry the following rudimentary spares on the car:

- **Fan belt**. While you can carry a proper replacement fan belt for your type of car, it's sometimes a fiddle to fit it, particularly if you're bending over the car in a downpour. Accessory shops sell a useful emergency belt, which you cut to length, according to the instructions, with a blade supplied with the belt, and then clip together. This is only a get-you-home dodge, but it can be fitted in minutes.

- **Set of lamp bulbs**. Many manufacturers provide a service kit of lamp bulbs, containing one of each type on the vehicle — head-lamps, sidelamps, rear/brake lights and indicators. If you drive with missing lights, not only is it dangerous but you're liable very quickly to attract the attention of the constables.

- **Emergency windscreen**. This is available as a roll of plastic, which you can fit in the unfortunate circumstances of your windscreen's shattering.

- **Set of fuses**. The owner's handbook will specify where your car's fusebox is and what kinds of fuses are fitted to it.

- **Can of oil**. Carry a good multigrade made by a reputable manu-facturer, or one approved by the makers of your car.

ROUTINE MAINTENANCE

While car-makers have always preferred that the reputation of their products be protected by skilled servicing, they have never assumed that the owner-driver would die rather than lift the bonnet. Some rudimentary checks need to be made on the car far more frequently than at service intervals, and you need to be aware of symptoms or signals the machine is putting out if you're not to ignore a cry for help that will eventually turn into a terminal illness.

Start by familiarizing yourself with where everything is on the car. It's astonishing how many owners who have a rough idea of what removing and recharging a battery means, actually turn out to have no idea where to look for it when the device finally gives up the ghost. Using the owner's handbook, locate the distributor, the ignition coil, the battery, the carburettor and the electric fuseboard.

Now look at the owner's handbook to determine what jobs they recommend you regularly carry out yourself. There are some that you should make a point of carrying out **weekly**. At the least these will be:

★ **Checking the battery**. This means unscrewing the caps or prising the plastic cover off the battery, and peering inside to ensure that the level of electrolyte is above the level of the rows of thin metal plates you'll see inside. **Don't smoke while you're doing this, or perform the examination using a naked light or there's likely to be an explosion**. Don't improvise by topping up with tap-water either, but always use distilled water. If the clamps holding the leads to the battery look very dirty or are covered in a greenish corrosion, loosen the clamp bolts with a suitable spanner, thoroughly clean the insides of the clamps and the battery posts, then put a dab of Vaseline around the posts and tighten everything up again. This will prevent corrosion from returning to the terminals, and minimize the starting problems caused by poor connections at the battery.

★ **Checking the oil, water, hydraulic fluid and windscreen washer levels**. You check the **oil** by removing the dip-stick on the side of the engine, wiping it clean, reinserting it (make sure it goes all the way down, or you won't get an accurate reading) and then withdrawing it again and comparing the level with the markings on the stick — which will usually specify a 'Max' and a 'Min'. Don't make this check within seconds of the engine stopping, because the oil takes a little while to drain back into the sump, and don't do it with the car parked on a slope either, or the reading will be distinctly misleading.

If the reading is close to the 'Min' or below it, top up the oil through the filler cap on the top of the engine, which should be clearly marked. Don't let the oil run low, or tell yourself you'll fix it next week, because not attending to a lack of lubrication is the surest way of wrecking the engine once you put your foot down. And if you find that the oil-level is dropping regularly, examine the engine for external leaks. If the engine isn't leaking then it's burning the oil, which you or those following you will notice because of an impressive cloud of blue smoke. It may be helpful if you're trying to throw off pursuers, but it doesn't endear you to the average road-user.

The **water-level** is checked with the engine cold. Once again, look for the details in the handbook. Modern cooling systems don't lose water that overflows through expansion but catch it in a bottle and return it to the radiator. This type shouldn't need topping up unless something's wrong with it, so you don't need to inspect the water-level in the radiator so frequently. If you have an older car with a conventional radiator cap, remove this and bring the water level up to within an inch of the neck of the inlet. **Don't** remove the radiator cap on a hot engine without protecting your hand and keeping your head out of the way, because you may get a spectacular geyser of scalding water in your face if you do.

Consult the handbook as to the whereabouts of the **hydraulic reservoirs**. There will certainly be one for the braking system, usually under the bonnet although in some older cars they can turn up in more awkward positions, such as under removable plates on the floor. The treacly-looking stuff inside should be at the level recommended in the book or marked on the side of the reservoir. If it's dropped, top it up with whatever type of fluid is endorsed in the handbook, and then **find out why it's leaking**.

Later in the book, we go into more detail about how you might do this, but if you don't want to develop your practical skills much beyond the present level of familiarity with where the bits are and what they do, you should take the car to a service station at once and have the fault diagnosed. Leaking hydraulic fluid in the brakes **can kill you, or somebody else**, if a neglected leak suddenly turns into a major loss of pressure. Although many modern cars now have fail-safe systems which prevent all four wheels from losing their braking action at once, you should **never ignore brake-fluid loss** whatever kind of car you have. Don't ever re-use old fluid for topping up, and don't drop fluid on the paintwork because it's highly corrosive.

The car may also have a hydraulic reservoir for the **clutch**, though many clutches are still operated by simple levers or cables. If there is one, keep it topped up in the same way, and regard loss of fluid from it with equal caution. If the clutch fails it's not as potentially disastrous as fluid loss from the brakes, but it can immobilize the car.

Also check the water-level in the **screen-washer bottle**, at the rear as well as the front if you have a rear-window-washer. Adding a small quantity of detergent to it is helpful.

Also in your weekly check, you should look at the tyre pressures (check the spare as well) using the gauge attached to your pump, and test the operation of all your lights and indicators, getting a friend to help you check the brake lights.

Your car is an investment, and one that suffers severely from depreciation, unless it's some kind of classic. It's therefore in your interests to forestall the effects of wear and tear and the elements at every possible opportunity. Maintaining it cosmetically doesn't merely keep you from looking like a slob in the eyes of your neighbours (and stop people writing 'Clean Me' and worse suggestions in the road-dirt on your battered hack) but also helps prevent far more serious and long-term deterioration from setting in.

First, it's sensible to keep it clean. Taking it to the local car-wash is the simplest course, but the brushes are not as kind to the paintwork as you will be with a bucket, a sponge and a chamois-leather. Keep the windows and windscreen clear too, for everybody's safety. Keeping it clean also, unfortunately, means clean in all those nasty places underneath where wet mud can lodge and eventually start eating away the metalwork. If you can really convince yourself you're going to undertake this onerous task from time to time, fine. If you suspect that the spirit may be willing but the flesh not quite up to it, take the car to a garage that has a **steamcleaner**. This blasts all the muck off with a high-pressure steam jet, and incidentally makes any work that you or anyone else has to do under the car a less depressing exercise.

Watch out for blemishes or small rust-spots on the paintwork. Any unprotected metal surface, however small, that is exposed to the air will quickly rust and the rust will spread under the good paintwork and eventually affect a much wider area that will be a lot harder to put right. Doing bodywork repairs to quite substantial damage or holes is a skill in itself and one that we outline later on, but for the purposes of simple maintenance, you need merely follow the instructions that the makers of your materials include on their packaging.

These amount to the following operations: if you have a rust-spot anywhere, first rub it down with abrasive paper, which the accessory shop will also supply. Make sure that you really do rub down to bright metal, even if this seems drastic and means rubbing away what looks like some good paintwork around the blemish. Once you're satisfied with the rubbing-down, apply the rust-killer, which will eat its way into any pitting where the rust has penetrated the metal and neutralize it. Leave it to dry for however long its maker suggests. If the area is very small — a patch smaller than your little fingernail, or simply a narrow scratch — you might then be able to get away with just carefully painting the area with the paint in the pot using the tiny brush that comes with it. If it's bigger, the operation may be a little more complex. You will need either to apply a **cellulose putty**, which is a kind of primer the consistency of butter, or to paint straight on to it if the surface looks smooth enough to you.

It's a characteristic of car gloss paints that they aren't thick enough to disguise imperfections, so the surface underneath needs to be really good. If you do use the cellulose putty, apply it with a rubber pad in very thin layers, let it dry and rub it down with wet-and-dry abrasive paper. You may then need to use two stages of aerosol spraying — first, a primer-filler, which is likely to be grey or white, and then the top coat once the primer is dry and you've given it a light rub-down with wet-and-dry paper of something like grade 400. Do mask off the surrounding area with masking tape and newspaper, though, or you'll get a fine mist of primer into all kinds of places where you don't want it.

DRIVING OBLIGATIONS

By now you will have organized yourself to satisfy most of the legal requirements that face you when you take a car on the road. The vehicle you've bought should now be insured for you to use, and for anybody else that you're likely to entrust it to, and be taxed for use on the public highways. You should possess a registration document for it, an insurance certificate and you may need a current certificate of roadworthiness — which in Britain is called the MOT test certificate. If you're the kind of person who wastes most of a day turning out drawers and pulling up carpets to find these things when you need them, then you're strongly advised to put them in a file or an envelope and keep them somewhere safe — but not in the car itself, because if anybody steals it you'll have made their life a great deal easier. The police can request scrutiny of all these items if they stop you on the road (though they will normally give you time to produce them later at a police station) and you have to produce them whenever you re-tax the car.

THE MOT TEST

This test is applied once a year to all cars over three years old. Not all garages are authorized to carry out MOT tests, and the ones that are will display the characteristic white triangle advertising the service. If the garage that services your car is also an MOT testing station then this obligation isn't much of a problem. If the garage isn't, you might nevertheless want them to give the car a pre-test check, and perhaps also to arrange to take the car to the testing station and back to minimize the running around you have to do.

The test takes in the following areas:

- **Lighting**. This means that all the lights, including the brake lights and indicators, must be working, in the correct positions and without their plastic lenses broken or discoloured. The dip or anti-dazzle beam of the headlights will be checked for alignment.

- **Steering and suspension**. This will take in all the steering controls and linkage, the transmission shafts of front-drive cars, the axles, wheel bearings, suspension joints and springing and the shock-absorbers. Wear, loose nuts and bolts and leaking hydraulics will all be failure points.

- **Brakes**. The condition, the efficiency and the balance of all the brakes will be measured on a special meter. Leaks, grabbing brakes or unequal braking effort at all the wheels will fail the car.

- **Tyres and wheels**. General tyre condition will be checked, with failure for cuts in the rubber, bulges or wear of the tread depth below 1 mm. The wheels themselves shouldn't be damaged or corroded badly enough to be weakened, and the stud holes where they are bolted to the hubs shouldn't be worn out of shape.

- **Seat belts**. The soundness of the mountings and the condition and freedom from fraying of the belts themselves will be examined.

- **The tester will also look at the windscreen-wipers and washers, the horn, the exhaust and the bodywork**. In the case of the latter, any serious structural weakness, particularly near power-unit or suspension mountings, and any dangerously loose or flapping bits will be a black mark for the car.

In the rest of this chapter, we will be outlining what's supposed to be done, either by yourself or by a professional, to keep the average car happily ticking away for thousands of miles. In the course of it, all the points just itemized for the statutory roadworthiness test will arise and we'll be telling you how to stop problems and suggesting things you can do to rectify them.

First of all, it should be reiterated that regular servicing, whether the car is working badly or working like a dream, is the foundation-stone of a motor car's longevity. If you neglect it on the grounds that nothing's wrong, the car's performance will slowly deteriorate in ways you might barely notice at first, and in the end there'll be a major breakdown — and whether this turns out to be a mild inconvenience, a bad shock or a terrible tragedy will be purely a matter of luck. So here's the rule: **Find out what the recommended service intervals for your car are, what's supposed to be done at them, and NEVER miss a service out**.

Cars hitting the market-place now require much less maintenance than formerly. In the days of lower overheads and labour costs, high-maintenance cars were not considered a liability. Sophisticated advances in lubrication technology have meant that nowadays moving parts are well protected over much higher mileages, while sealed-for-life components have reduced the need for what used to be rather disparagingly called the grease-monkey, and electronics are replacing mechanical devices for such systems as the car's ignition. While all this is a boon to the busy driver, it does of course mean that the car gets the once-over less often than it used to, so when something does start to go wrong, it may no longer be caught at an early stage.

The car's makers will none the less have determined what its service intervals should be, and you should discover these and what jobs are itemized for each service. At the base service, items to be looked at are likely to include:

- **Engine**. Change the engine oil, top up any carburettor damper systems (see page 136) and check the generator and water-pump belts.

- **Ignition**. Check and clean the sparking plugs, reset the electrode gap (see page 127), check the contact points, clean and reset.

- **Clutch**. Check the setting of the clutch-release mechanism and adjust if applicable.

- **Steering and Suspension**. Check the tightness of all nuts and bolts, make sure the moving parts are free from wear and that there is no fluid leakage from the shock-absorbers, give attention to any grease points with the grease gun and check the condition of any rubber seals or gaiters on the steering or transmission joints.

- **Brakes**. Check the brake linings and/or disc pads and the condition of pipework and flexible hoses.

- In addition you should give attention to all the points we mentioned earlier as part of the weekly check-over.

Having listed above a lot of what might be incomprehensible projects, in the next chapter we shall try to simplify what they all mean. This may or may not lead you to undertake some of these jobs yourself (though with only a modest expansion of the fairly rudimentary tool-kit itemized at the start of the chapter you would be able to perform most service tasks without too much trouble)', but at least it will give you an idea of what the mechanic you're paying good money to is supposed to be up to.

6

A SECOND OPINION

' "Well, good god" he said "you just backed over that two-foot
concrete abutment and you didn't even slow down! Forty-five
in reverse! And you barely missed the pump!"
"No harm done" I said. "I always test a transmission that way.
The **rear end**. For stress factors." '
(Hunter S. Thompson, Fear and Loathing in Las Vegas)

In the last chapter we looked at what motor manufacturers expect their products to need in the way of tender loving care. It's likely that you'll try to find someone you can trust to do this work for you, or have it taken care of by the agents for the model you have. Some of the work is certainly straightforward enough for even novices to contemplate doing themselves, with a modicum of attention to detail and thoroughness, and we would certainly recommend that those who don't feel too faint at the thought should consider it. You might do just enough to realize that getting dirty fingernails and lying in the gutter is simply never going to be your cup of tea, but you might also do just enough to gain confidence in the idea that rescuing yourself or someone else from a breakdown is possible and gratifying. And if you get that far, then doing your own regular routine servicing is just a small step away.

For the moment though, we'll assume that you don't want to go any further than understanding the language people use to discuss your car, working out for yourself where all the bits and pieces that this vocabulary applies to are, and getting some idea as to whether the professionals are doing what they say they're doing. Even going just this far will entail getting a bit dirty, and frequenting yourself with some elementary safety precautions. Points to bear in mind are:

★ **Cleanliness**. Many people are put off messing about with cars because the state it leaves your hands in is unlikely to endear you to that special friend you're meeting later on. That nauseated gaze as you entwine fingers over the brandy may be a price you'd rather not pay for self-sufficiency.

You can't get round this problem completely, which is an unfortunate fact of motoring life — but you can improve things by using a barrier cream before you plunge in and a good proprietary hand-cleansing gel afterwards (we're talking about the car now, not the friend), and if you aren't going to do too much fiddly dismantling but just a kind of general reconnaissance, then you might find that a pair of rubber gloves does the trick instead. Rubber gloves are not ideal for doing serious work on the car, because the lack of sensation is a handicap and contact with metal parts quickly rips them up, but they're fine for just feeling your way, as it were.

★ **Fire**. Whatever you do, **don't smoke**. You may well visit garages in which phlegmatic artisans are bending over carburettors with dog-ends hanging out of their mouths, but it's crazy to do it. And if you're lucky enough to be able to keep your car under cover, remember that you're not supposed to store in the garage any petrol except what the vehicle has in its tank, and a spare can of petrol in the boot — and the spare can should be steel, not plastic.

★ **Other injuries**. If you have **long hair**, tie it out of the way, particularly if you're looking into the engine compartment while the motor is running. Hair getting caught in fast-moving machinery is a very common and nasty form of industrial accident, and there's no reason why it shouldn't happen to you either. Remove jewellery like rings, watches and bracelets. **Don't** breathe in the dust found in brake parts and clutches if you get involved in serious dismantling — it may contain asbestos. **Never** run the engine in an enclosed space unless you're venting the poisonous exhaust fumes through a pipe to the outside. **Don't** open the radiator cap while the engine's very hot or you might scald yourself. **Don't** spill the fluid from the battery over yourself or over clothes or paintwork.

And at the risk of labouring the point, we reiterate the warnings about getting underneath. You can't come to much harm wriggling under a vehicle if it isn't raised off the ground (as long as it isn't parked on a slope and you're sure the handbrake is on), but if you raise the car, **never go under it** if it's supported only on a jack. Good quality axle stands or ramps should be used to support it.

SERVICE TASKS

Taking routine servicing first, because this is the type of encounter with a garage you're most likely to experience, unless you're unlucky enough to have a major breakdown. Services are the tasks that any car manufacturer is going to regard as fundamental in order to keep the vehicle safe, efficient, reliable and likely to survive its proper life-span. We're assuming here that you want to be familiar with what the garage is expected to do at service intervals, and to have some idea of how to check that everything has been done.

If, on the other hand, the car is displaying signs of some major upset to its system — such as inexplicable mechanical noise from the engine or transmission, substantial loss of performance or clouds of smoke — then clearly you will be expecting the garage's service to include attention to whatever is causing this. Or if it starts happening only *after* the car returns from service, you will want to know why. Later in the book we include extensive fault-finding information to help you pin-point some of these undesirable occurrences, but the purpose of the coming pages is to help you develop a relationship of mutual respect with your garage in the context of more routine operations.

★ **Lubrication**. Oil changes are crucial to prolonged engine life. The owner's handbook will specify the oil-change intervals and maybe even a grade or type of oil that the makers regard as ideal for the car.

Your garage should change the oil with the car warmed up, so that the oil is fluid enough to drain off effectively. It is drained by the removal of the **sump drain plug**, the whereabouts of which will probably be specified in the handbook. You're sure to find it in the lowest part of the sump, which is the deep metal tray bolted to the underside of the engine.

Why does the oil have to be replaced so frequently? Is it a conspiracy by the Gulf States, a global scam secured by massive back-handers between the oil industry and the motor business? After all, the old stuff may look a bit on the mucky side, but it's still slippery enough, which you may discover if you're unlucky enough to spill it on the floor. The problem is that every gallon of petrol burned in the engine produces a gallon of water as a by-product. Most of this leaves the engine as steam, but some gets into the oil and, as they say, 'emulsifies' it, which is another way of saying that it forms a sludge. The desirability of discouraging this sludge is the reason why you hear oil-company advertising going on so much about the 'detergent' effects of their products. And undeniably, modern multigrade oils have an extremely powerful detergent effect, which is what is now lengthening the oil-change intervals.

Possibly at the same intervals, or longer ones, the makers will recommend the changing of the **oil filter**. As you might remember from our consideration of the engine and its habits, the filter is a canister containing a blotting-paper-like material. The blotting-paper part can be renewed and the canister bolted back, or the whole can is scrapped and a replacement fitted. The garage should replace this item at the recommended intervals, and do the job without creating oil leaks through loose joints in the process. You can, however, perform a rudimentary visual check yourself.

Oil filters are often in awkward places on the engine but are usually set low on one or other side of the crankcase. If the garage has done what it says it's done, the filter body shouldn't be covered in a thick film of grease or look as if it hasn't been touched for years. Certainly if the filter is the throwaway type — do establish this from

the handbook first before you get into an embarrassing row —
you'll have a nice gleaming and spotless new filter in place when the
car comes back from service, and if you haven't, you should check
your invoice to see if you've been charged for one, and either way
you should ask what's going on.

Though the garage should check them, it's sensible and no trouble to maintain your own check on any rubber belts the engine has.
There may be one pulley driving the water pump and generator, or
there may be two. Whichever is the case, press the belt (or belts)
down with your finger in the middle of its longest run. There
shouldn't be more than about a centimetre of give in it — if there's
more, then the belt tension needs to be adjusted according to the
instructions in the handbook. This usually involves slackening the
pivot bolts on the generator so that the whole unit can be pulled
further out to a position where the belt is tighter, then retightening
the pivot bolts without letting it slip back. Don't over-tension the
belt though, and examine it for cracks, oil-impregnation or fraying.

IGNITION

Ignition systems are the bane of motorists and motoring rescue
organizations. Ignition failures lurk behind a high proportion of
breakdowns on the road — many of which could have been avoided
if there had been proper maintenance in the first place. Of all the
components on a car likely to manifest their dissatisfaction at neglect, the ignition system will probably do it first, and with the most
infuriating consequences.

You shouldn't have too much of a problem working out where
the distributor is, since it's the inverted-cup-shaped object with all
the wires going to the sparking plugs sprouting out of it, and it will
be sitting on the side of the engine somewhere. Take a look at page
18 in Chapter Two to familiarize yourself with the ignition system
and what its various bits and pieces do.

The service station will attend to the ignition by cleaning the
plugs and setting the sparking-plug gap to the correct measurement,
or ditching the plugs and replacing them if necessary. If you're
really paranoid about your garage, you could mark your sparking
plugs with some code that you'll be familiar with (a small spot of
paint on the ceramic part for instance) as a double check that
they've replaced the plugs when they say they have. Part of any
service should also be a check on the distributor's **contact-breaker
points** (hereinafter called 'the points'), the **condenser**, and the
ignition timing.

Checking whether or not these jobs have been done will require a modicum of dismantling, so a word of warning first. As you should now appreciate from the explanatory chapter dealing with the ignition, it's crucial that there is synchronization of the sparking of the plugs with the movements of the pistons and valves. In other words, if you disconnect the leads from the sparking plugs and reconnect them in the wrong order, very strange things will happen and the car will either not start at all, or sound very unhappy if it does. So **if you pull more than one sparking plug lead off the plugs at any one time, label the lead so you know which plug it goes back to**.

Leave the plug leads connected for the moment and pull back the two spring clips that hold the plastic distributor cap on to the metal body of the component. Then lift the cap off. Underneath you will see the distributor rotor, and below that the contact points. Lift the rotor off the spindle (it may just be a stiff push-fit, with a lug and a cut-away section on the spindle to ensure proper relocation, or it may have a screw or two) so that you can get a better view of the points.

You can assess the condition of your points — or ascertain whether you've been fitted with new ones or not — by pushing the sprung contacts apart with your index finger whilst shining the flashlight on them and getting your peepers fairly close up to the problem. The working faces of contact points are tiny circular metal blocks not much more than a couple of millimetres in diameter, so you do need to be able to get a good view. If they've been cleaned and reset, or if they've been renewed, the two little circles should be moderately bright. Points that have been in service for a long time look worn, eaten away by sparking, and there is likely to be a raised 'pip' on one contact breaker and a corresponding recess in the other one. Also, on the moving arm of the contacts there is a plastic or fibre 'heel' that bears on the spindle cams in the centre of the distributor. Remember from Chapter Two that as the cams rotate, they flip the fibre heel up and down and alternately open and close the points. There should be a small smear of clean grease at this point following a service.

Now look inside the distributor cap, particularly at the brass contacts. The contacts should be clean and bright and not eaten away or encrusted with greenish corrosion, and there should be no dark lines running across the inside of the cap and forming a bridge from one contact to another. The latter phenomenon is known as 'tracking' — the dark lines are little rivers of carbon, and they indicate a form of short circuit in which the spark is jumping from one terminal to another along the track instead of going where it should do. If your distributor is suffering from this disease, then the whole cap will have to be renewed.

Whilst examining the distributor cap make sure that the contact in the *centre* of it — usually a little black carbon brush on a coil spring, but sometimes a flat metal spring arm — works freely and has a reasonable amount of springiness in it so that it bears effectively on to the rotor.

You won't be able to check the ignition timing yourself unless you're prepared to throw yourself a bit more seriously into grappling with the car, which we go into a little later. Suffice to say at this stage that errors in the ignition timing may account for:

★ **Hard starting.**

★ **'Pinking'** — which is a high-pitched metallic-sounding noise on hard acceleration, which seems to be a suggestion that something vital in the engine is actually loose or wearing out, but isn't that at all. We described earlier how not only did the ignition system have to get the spark to arrive at the right point in the engine's cycle, but also that 'right point' changed according to the car's engine speed and the work it was having to do. If the distributor is not 'advancing' the spark correctly — in other words, making it happen progressively earlier in the cycle as the engine speed rises, or retarding it if the load is heavy — then you'll hear the engine 'pinking' in protest, which means that the explosion of gas is happening too suddenly and not in a progressive, power-delivering manner. If you find your car doing this after a service, take it back. And don't drive it at prolonged high speeds, such as on a motorway, whilst the engine is pinking, or severe damage to the engine could result.

★ **Poor acceleration.**

There may be a number of other related faults caused by timing problems, including overheating and plug damage.

Routine servicing will also involve attention to the **carburettor**. This is not an instrument that's particularly amenable to double-checks on your garage's standards, and the best idea you can get as to whether it's being looked after lies in the performance of the car.

You can, however, get the beginnings of an understanding of the carburettor by referring once again to the owner's handbook, and to our summary of what the carburettor does, on page 27. The handbook will specify what kind of carburettor it is, inform you as to whether it's the kind of **variable-jet** carburettor that requires its piston damper to be topped up with engine oil, and in all probability tell you where the adjusting screws are. In more old-fashioned carburettors, there is a provision for adjustment of both the **idling speed**, which is the speed at which the engine turns over when you have your foot off the accelerator pedal, and of the **mixture**, which is the proportion of petrol to air. Modern fuel systems restrict the scope for owner-adjustment to the idling speed, and the makers tend to insist that any further changes are only made by a dealer with the right equipment. In order further to discourage breaches of these arrangements, they often cover over or seal any other adjusting screws.

The reasons for this are not entirely because the makers are spoilsports or they're trying to make money for the agents. As the number of cars on the world's roads continues to rise, and attention given to the dangers of pollution rises with it, higher standards have come to be applied to the kinds of junk that motor cars are allowed to hurl into the atmosphere. Whereas in the past carburettors would be adjusted by canny old pros who would do it by listening to the engine note and sampling the exhaust, nowadays very sophisticated electronic instruments capable of measuring the quantities of the various components of the exhaust gas are used instead. Manufacturers supply strict recommendations as to what percentages of what should be in the exhaust, and agents are supposed to set carburettors up accordingly.

However, the following considerations are worth remembering in the context of carburettors:

Fuel consumption. This can fairly easily be roughly estimated. The owner's handbook will specify the capacity of the fuel tank and you should fill it, make a note of your mileage reading on the speedometer, drive the car until the gauge reaches its 'half-full' point, then divide the mileage you've covered by whatever figure a half-tank of petrol is on your car to get an idea of how many miles you're doing to the gallon/litre. The figure will always be lower on stop–start town driving than on long runs, but if the consumption seems to be excessive this may be a sign of maladjustment of the carburettor. Also look out for:

Hard starting, uneven performance, power shortage, stalling. The reasons for these faults are not always associated with the fuel system, but when they are it can be because one (or more) of the jets is blocked by dirt, the float chamber (the carburettor's 'cistern') has its level wrongly set or its valve is faulty, the fuel pump is weak, or there's an air leak where the carburettor is joined to the engine.

Petrol smells. If you smell petrol in or around the car when it isn't running, suspect leaks in the tank or the fuel-lines. If you smell it at idle, the fuel pipe between the pump and the carburettor may be leaking, or the carburettor float chamber overflowing. **Don't check with a naked light**.

As part of any service, the garage should check the operation of the carburettor for all these faults — either electronically or manually. And if the instrument is of the variable-jet type we mentioned above, they should top up the damper as well. As part of your regimen of gently taking simple things apart to break the alien untouchableness of the car, unscrew the damper yourself if your carburettor happens to be of this type — the handbook will tell you where to find it — and check that the tube the damper screws into is two-thirds full of oil.

Transmission and running-gear servicing. The service station will also check the condition and operation of the clutch and gearbox (or automatic transmission if your car is so equipped), the steering, suspension, brakes and lights.

If your car is equipped with a conventional clutch (in other words, you have a separate clutch pedal), start by figuring out where the various bits of it go. A transverse-engined, front-drive car will have its clutch housing — a big, bell-shaped cowling — close to one or other of the front wings. About half-way down it, and on the end of a shaft running horizontally through the housing, will be the **clutch operating lever**. Linked to this will be a rod — possibly activated by a small hydraulic cylinder — or a cable that runs back through the bulkhead of the car and into the driver's compartment. The end of this rod is likely to be threaded and have one or two nuts on it. In a front-engined, rear-drive car where the engine is aligned front-to-back rather than transversely, the clutch housing is likely to be more inaccessible and the lever and adjuster underneath the vehicle, but you should be able at least to get sight of it without raising the car, by wriggling under with a torch.

Having worked out what goes where, check in the owner's handbook about clutch adjustment. On many cars there is a degree of slack, usually around ¾ inch, as you begin to depress the clutch pedal, before you start to feel the resistance of the springs or diaphragm within the clutch. If there's no play at all, you may already be noticing the phenomenon known as 'clutch slip' (see page 168) as you drive, whereby the engine speed appears to be rising fast but the car isn't progressing with the same enthusiasm. And if there's much more than an inch of play before you start to feel the resistance, then you may be noticing that gear changes are noisy or you have trouble getting into first and reverse. Either way, these are conditions that the service station should correct by adjusting the clearance between the operating rod or cable and the release mechanism that is part of the clutch itself.

Eventually, following one of these manipulations, the garage will say that there's no room for any further adjustment and that you will need an expensive new clutch. Unless some component of the clutch has actually broken, which is unusual, the reason will be that there is no further scope for adjustment on the operating rod or cable. You can check this by ascertaining whether the adjusting nuts on the threaded part of the cable or rod are now at the end of their travel. If you are told by the garage that a new clutch is necessary, get a quote for the job, and an estimate of how long you'll be giving up the car for. Chains of establishments devoted only to doing high-speed clutch, gearbox and exhaust replacements are opening new branches all the time. The good ones will guarantee their work, often be cheaper than a regular garage, and complete the job very quickly, sometimes even while you wait. Make sure though, that opting for such a service doesn't invalidate any guarantee you already have on the car.

STEERING AND SUSPENSION

It can't be overemphasized that proper checks on the steering and suspension, and prompt correction of any faults, are the most vital forms of attention your car can receive. There are severe limitations on what you can achieve yourself by way of servicing these components, because work on them often requires special equipment. But you can at least double-check what you would expect your garage to be keeping an eye on so that if you're the nervous type you might spend fewer nights waking up and worrying about your ball joints. Naturally these checks are a bit anti-social because they involve grovelling about in the dirt underneath.

Once again, you have to start by working out what sort of suspension system your car has. Remember from Chapter Three (page 48) that a pair of roadwheels can be **independently** suspended, or a solid **beam axle** with a wheel at either end can be suspended from the frame as a unit.

It would be helpful, as in many spheres, if at least there were a standardized way of going about the work, but the sad fact is that suspension systems vary. In some independent arrangements the roadwheel is attached on an upper and a lower arm, each hinged to the bodywork, and with a coil spring mounted between either the lower or the upper arm and the body. (Remember that while they're called arms, they're actually pretty bulky items, and may look more of a triangular shape, the hinged end being at the 'base' and the wheel mounting at the 'apex'.) A **Macpherson strut** system has only a lower hinged arm, from which a strut with a coil spring on the end of it passes more or less vertically upwards and joins the upper body direct, just under each front wing. At the rear of the car, a similar system may exist if the design pursues the modern tendency towards independent suspension all round, or there may be a solid axle, possibly with leaf springs or torsion bars cushioning its movements, as we described on page 48.

The most common type of wear to front suspension systems takes place in the **ball joints**. As you can imagine, since the components of a front suspension system have to accommodate not only the up-and-down movement of road-shocks and bumps, but also the side-to-side movement involved in steering the car, the bits need to be joined together by something rather similar to what happens in your elbow. And just as the ball joints of people who have clocked up a high mileage can wear out, so it is with cars. The ball is machined to be a close fit in its socket, and the whole unit packed with a special grease. When it wears, the ball gets sloppy in the socket, and the handling of the car gets sloppy too, with symptoms such as wandering steering and a tendency for the car to swerve when braking.

In a conventional front suspension system, there will be ball joints where the part that the wheel and brake mechanism is bolted to (the **steering knuckle**) is linked to the upper and lower arms. In a Macpherson system, there will only be one ball joint. Each joint has a tapered section beneath the ball which passes through a corresponding hole in the steering knuckle, and is fastened with a nut on the other side. But not just any nut. Because it's so crucial that nothing in the steering suddenly comes apart, the nut will be 'locked' on to its thread in some way — usually by a device called a **split pin**, which passes through notches in the top of the nut, through a hole in the threaded taper and out of the other side, at which point each 'leg' of the split pin is folded back to lock the nut.

It should also be borne in mind that not all ball joints carry the same load. Look at the front suspension on your car, which you should be able to examine without lifting the vehicle — turning the steered wheels to one side will help. If the coil spring is fitted between the upper and the lower suspension arms, the lower ball joint is the more critical one. If the spring is fitted between the upper arm and the body, then the upper ball joint is load bearing.

To perform a check on the ball joints yourself, you merely have to repeat the examination that you may have had an opportunity to make when you bought the car. It requires a **scissors-jack** rather than a hydraulic bottle-jack because only the former can be retracted low enough to fit under one of the suspension units. Chock the rear wheels of the car, fit the jack under one of the lower suspension arms, and raise the wheel about two inches off the ground. Then get a friend to try to rock the roadwheel vertically back and forth. By shining a torch on the ball joints, and **without getting underneath** you should be able to see if there's any slack or free movement in the joint. Placing the jack under the lower arm will reveal play where the lower ball joint is the main load-carrier. Where the coil spring is above the upper arm, place the jack under a suitably robust-looking bit of the front body frame instead, and similarly waggle the wheel, this time shining your light on the upper ball joint.

While you're examining the suspension ball joints, you can also do the same for the steering. Let the car off the jack to begin with. Then locate the track-rods, which are the tubular sections linked to each steering knuckle — you can find them by lying at the front of the car and watching what moves as your partner turns the steering wheel from side to side. Whether you have a Pitman-type steering unit — in which worm gears are enclosed in a small box at the chassis end of the steering column — or the rack-and-pinion system we described on page 52, the roadwheel end of the arrangement will be the same. Start by setting the roadwheels in the straight-ahead position, and then grasp the **drop arm**, which is the short arm that protrudes from the bottom of a Pitman-type box, or one of the tie-rods if it's a rack-and-pinion type. Get your partner to move the steering wheel. There should be little or no free movement at the wheel, and if there is, it indicates wear in the steering gearbox or the rack-and-pinion mechanism.

Now locate each ball joint in the linkage and try to move it up and down — not rotationally. If there is vertical play, the joint needs to be scrapped and replaced. Similarly, if there is vertical play in the joints of the rod running from the steering box, these need to be replaced as well. While you're examining what goes on under the car, check the condition of any rubber coverings or 'gaiters' protecting the steering and suspension joints from dirt and sealing in the pre-packed grease. If these are torn, grease gets out and dirt gets in, and if this happens the joint won't survive for long. Also under the car, visually check the shock-absorbers for any signs of hydraulic-fluid leakage. If the owner's handbook specifies grease points that need attention from a grease gun, you should find that immediately following a service these points are clean, and have a smear of grease on them. If there are separate **drive shafts** rather than the enclosed type in a solid rear axle, these will also have rubber gaiters enclosing their joints, and these gaiters should similarly be examined for splits or damage.

Lastly, get as good a view as you can of the **brake-fluid pipes**. On independent suspensions, you will find a flexible hose running from pipe junctions on the bodywork to the back of each wheel. On solid axles, like the rear axles of many front-engined cars, there will probably be only one hose, running from a junction to the axle, with metal pipes conducting the fluid from there to each wheel. The hose shouldn't be chafed, cracking or in any way deteriorating, and the joints should betray no fluid leaks. If the garage has told you that it's replaced the flexible hoses, examine them for yourself. The condition of a new hose, its freedom from road-dirt and the cleanliness of its joints will be immediately obvious.

You can't check what attention has been given to drum brakes without doing more extensive dismantling, but check the brake-drums to ensure that there are no signs of hydraulic fluid weeping from them. On disc brakes, examine the disc itself — which should be polished and bright, free from score marks or abrasions — and the **brake pads** which are fitted to either side of the calliper (see page 56). The thickness of the pads should be no less than ⅛ inch, and if it is they should be replaced. New pads, if claimed to have been fitted by the garage, should once again be immediately obvious by their cleanliness and by the thickness of the friction material.

Dirt or lack of lubrication in steering parts may reveal itself in the form of stiff steering action, or squeaks when the wheels are turned. Don't confuse these symptoms with heavy steering, particularly at low speeds and when parking. Sometimes this is a characteristic of the design, but under-inflated tyres may also be contributing to the problem.

Other abnormalities in the handling of the car may be caused by problems in the suspension. If the steering **wanders**, this may also be due to incorrect tyre inflation. But it may be caused by looseness in the suspension parts, by the **steering geometry** (see page 53) being wrongly adjusted, or by a buckled wheel — the sort of thing you can get from banging the car unceremoniously against the kerb.

Wheel wobble is an unnerving condition, which will often reveal itself at high road speeds, sometimes occurring only in a particular speed range and not at other times. The service station should attend to the **wheel balance** regularly, and if you experience wheel wobble, incorrect balance will very probably be the reason for it. Having the steering geometry checked, as above, is also a sensible precaution. Wheel wobble can be caused by wear in the steering joints, but your earlier examination should have identified this.

Pitching, rolling, and sometimes **wheel tramp** (a condition in which judder at the back wheels is apparent during hard acceleration) can be caused by weakness of the springs or the shock-absorbers. Test for shock-absorber wear by exerting downward pressure on the wings of the car and observing whether the car immediately returns to its normal position when you release it, as it should, or whether it goes on bouncing — you may have done this already if you conducted your own examination before purchase, as in Chapter Four. This isn't an infallible test, but taken in conjunction with other oddities of handling in use, it gives a strong indication. For general spring wear and settlement, examine the car at front and rear for signs of sagging or listing to one side.

Thus prepared, you should have a better idea of what service stations are talking about, and be able to keep a better check on what they're up to and what you should expect of them.

You should also now be reasonably familiar with how your car works, at least in its fundamentals. In the next chapter we'll be looking at what you can do if you feel willing and able to progress a little further in taking matters into your own hands. Naturally, we would hope that you take this opportunity in the fullness of time, when you're good and ready. But the fates may decree that you'll be obliged to take this on sooner than you might want to.

We thus provide you, in the next chapter, with a guide to doing your own car servicing, exactly as the service station would do it, though without the benefit of sophisticated testing equipment. Although some problems may eventually force you to retreat for a check with this sort of equipment, much useful work can be done without such devices — as it has been in the motor trade for a hundred years. And in the chapter following that, we deal with emergency measures — how to rescue yourself or someone else from a roadside breakdown.

7

GETTING INVOLVED

*'Allan Vidow, who was a motor mechanic in civvy street,
thought that a streamlined car
looks very nice, but he considered that it should not be
necessary to suspend a mechanic feet uppermost,
and then lower him down head
first into the bonnet, which is almost
necessary to carry out maintenance on some cars now.'
(British POWs'* Mühlberg Motor Club *magazine,
Stalag 4B, 1944)*

In the last chapter we gave you some ideas as to how to follow what a service station does when you entrust your car to it, and how to keep track of whether the professionals are doing what they say they're doing. You may have got your hands dirty in that chapter, but mostly in getting familiar with the workings of your car rather than in actually removing any of its vitals for inspection.

Going this far may be as much as you'll need if you're convinced you will never want to do your own servicing, and that if you break down you'll ring for rescue and retire to the nearest hostelry. But if you do want to get to know the car more intimately, we shall describe in the next two chapters both how you can undertake routine servicing yourself and how you can get yourself out of a jam if you break down — as well as providing a brief run-down of what you should expect if you ever want to chance your arm into the field of even more major work.

Firstly, the service. Some of the following may seem to cover ground already examined in the last chapter, but at this stage of the game, it's time both to remind yourself of what we covered there and to gain some experience of what it feels like to wield the spanner yourself.

Begin by reacquainting yourself with the safety precautions listed on page 94. Then assess whether you're sufficiently well equipped.

TOOLS

You should be able to conduct a basic service with the tool-kit we recommended that you invest in at the outset, with some additions which we'll describe as we go along. But if you are going to do regular, thorough and safe work on your motor car, you need to have some equipment that you can support the raised vehicle on when you're going to work underneath. There are two alternatives. Using **axle stands** is one way of doing it. These are sturdy steel tripods, the central section of which can be raised or lowered to suit different levels of lift. You jack the car up, place the axle stands under a suitably rugged part of the underframe and secure it at the correct height, then lower the jack until the stand is carrying the weight — and you will normally need to lift the car on both sides at the same time, so that it's evenly raised to the same height at the front or the back, taking care that you chock the other pair of wheels to stop the vehicle rolling away.

Ramps are also available, and are easier to use, though they can be used only at a fixed height, and aren't suitable for jobs that involve both lifting and removing a wheel. You simply drive or reverse the car up the pair of steel ramps (getting an assistant to guide you on), then apply the handbrake and chock the wheels.

There is a further prop that is invaluable once you get into serious servicing. The owner's handbook for the car is a vital source of hints and advice, but it's intended only for those who wish merely to understand their car and its needs, and to attend only to its most basic necessities themselves. Once you go further, it's invaluable to furnish yourself with the **workshop manual** for your particular model. Several publishers now specialize in these tomes, and very often the research for them has been done by specialist motoring authors who have actually dismantled the vehicle in question themselves down to the last nut and bolt. So you don't get those blithe underestimates of the difficulties of performing a particular task. If the authors believe you're about to come up against a job fraught with unexpected snags, difficulties of access and likelihood of rusted bolts wrecking your optimistic declaration of 'this won't take a minute', they'll tell you. Workshop manuals aren't expensive, and they'll repay investment many times over — in terms of hard cash, time and mental energy. You may find, in the course of this chapter, that our frequent recommendations as to how you should consult the manual border on the tedious. We reiterate them only because all models are subtly different, and there is no substitute for specialist information.

And lastly, spare parts. Spares for popular production cars are now available in many kinds of stores, from highly respected high-street chains, via dubious-looking but honest motor factors to dubious-looking and dishonest ones. It has become increasingly common for manufacturers other than the original makers of the car to produce spares. Some of them are of high quality, others have much-reduced service lives or are even positively dangerous. The only safe policy — at the risk of our doing a disservice to some possibly reputable alternative sources — is to buy the manufacturers' approved parts from their agencies, or to make sure that you're getting a brand-name substitute from a well-known manufacturer. Counterfeiting parts is becoming quite a lucrative industry, but it causes nothing but headache and increased risks for the consumer. You may in an emergency be forced to use a spare from another source, but don't chance it in the case of parts for those crucial areas of car safety — particularly the steering, the suspension and the brakes.

If you're going to undertake a standard service, begin with your new companion, the manual, and make a list of the tasks that are required at the service interval — which nowadays will usually be 5000–6000 miles, or once a year if you do less mileage than that. If you live in a country that has a statutory roadworthiness test like the British MOT, it might be labour-saving to combine your big service and check-up with the pre-test preparations.

Begin with a check of the cooling system, because it's preferable to do this before you start up the engine. In the cooling-system part of the routine weekly check we mentioned that if your car was of the sealed type with an expansion tank to catch and recycle overflows then it didn't need such regular attention (page 87). Nevertheless, the system does need some systematic examination. A United States Department of Transportation survey showed that cooling-system failures are the third most common cause of breakdowns on the road, because it is the kind of system that is ignored if it's not causing any trouble.

At the service intervals the levels in the system should certainly be checked, but only when the engine is cool. Remove the cap on the radiator by pressing it down and twisting it off. The water-level should be very nearly at the top of the neck of the inlet. If it isn't, top it up, run the engine to warm it up again, let it cool down and then recheck the level — a sequence you should also adopt if the system has been drained down, to replenish the antifreeze for instance. Go on repeating it until there's no further change in the water-level.

A further check to make before you get the engine hot is to examine the condition of the rubber pipework. Using a flashlight look for seepage of water from pipe joints, look for any areas where incorrect mounting of components may be causing metalwork to be chafing against rubber pipes, and take care — if the manual records that your car is fitted with one — that you locate the small bypass pipe near the water pump, which may also be causing inconspicuous trouble. Squeeze the pipework with your hand. It should feel pliable but firm, and spring quickly back into shape. If it's excessively spongy or excessively hard (possibly with brittleness implying incipient failure) then the pipe should be replaced. If you're going to replace it, you will need the manual to help you locate the taps or drain plugs of the engine so that you can drain off the water. Then undo the worm-drive clips with a screwdriver, remove the old pipe and substitute a correct replacement. Top up the radiator with a mixture of antifreeze and water mixed in the proportions recommended by the antifreeze manufacturer.

Now move on to the **oil change**. The engine must be warm for the old oil to be effectively drained off. You then need to get under the car to find the drain plug, which will be somewhere in the base of the sump. You should be able to reach the sump plug without needing to raise the car. Make sure you have the right-sized spanner — or if necessary any special wrench required by the design, and almost certainly specified in the handbook — and that you're attempting to rotate the plug in the right direction to undo it. Loosen the plug, but before you extract it altogether, place a bowl or tray underneath the sump, reminding yourself first of the capacity of the sump so that you don't get an overflow. Then unscrew the plug and let the oil drain off, and leave it for some minutes after the bulk of it has flowed out for the last drips to emerge. Clean the plug, screw it finger tight into the hole and tighten it up fully with the spanner. You should make sure that you apply a modicum of pressure to the spanner, but don't break out in a sweat doing it or you may do it up so tight that you strip the threads in the sump, which would be highly inconvenient, to say the least. Stow the discarded oil in an old screw-top can and check out your local authority's recommendations about its disposal. Lubricating oil should *not* be poured down a drain.

Then comes replacement of the **oil filter**, which should accompany all oil changes. The **replaceable-element** type usually has to be unbolted from beneath the car, and once again, like the oil change, you should be able to do it without needing to lift the body. The throwaway type can more often be reached from the top. With the replaceable-element type, a long bolt usually passes vertically up from the base of the filter and you need to remove this to pull the canister out. Ease it out carefully, and put a tray underneath to catch the splashes — the canister itself will be full of oil, so don't wave it about or the evidence of your performance of this task will be writ large all over you.

In the box with the replacement filter there is likely to be a rubber ring like a thick elastic band, which is intended to seal the joint between the canister and the housing bolted to the engine. It makes sense to leave the old one in if it hasn't been leaking, because grovelling around in the gutter you can find it a fiddly item to replace. Clean out the canister inside and out, place the new filter element in it (remember to take note of any instructions as to which way up it should be) and push the whole lot squarely back into place so that the rim of the casing fits properly into the lip on the upper part. Then replace the retaining bolt and tighten it up. Start the engine and watch for leaks. If it does leak, slightly slacken the bolt, reposition the filter casing, tighten up and try again. If it still leaks, then the old rubber ring will need to be dug out with something like a fine electrical-screwdriver blade, the new one carefully and evenly fitted to the groove, and the whole lot reassembled.

With the throwaway type of filter, quite a lot of this fiddling about is bypassed. The can isn't amenable to dismantling, but screws in

REPLACING THE OIL FILTER

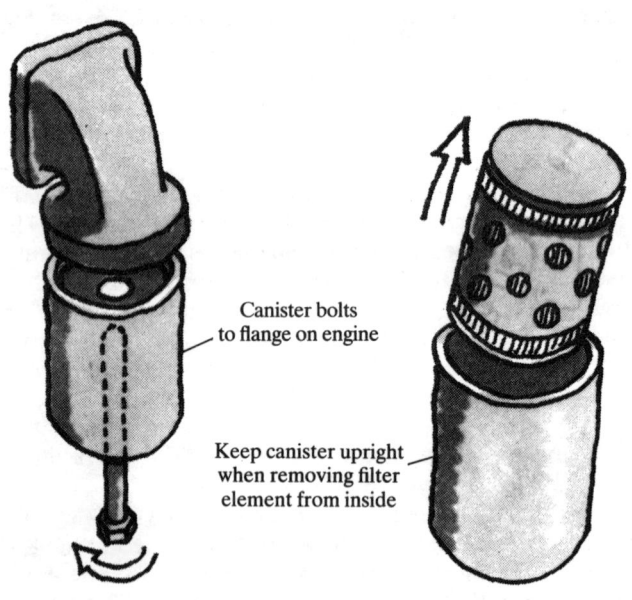

Canister bolts to flange on engine

Keep canister upright when removing filter element from inside

one piece on to the side of the engine. Removing it can be done either by using a **filter wrench** — which is the correct tool, resembling a length of bicycle chain, and which is wound around the filter body and pulls itself tight — or by puncturing the old filter with a hammer and cold chisel and hitting it anticlockwise to start unscrewing it. When you screw on the new one, check out the condition of any rubber rings or seals at the joint. Once you're sure everything's secure, refill the engine with the recommended lubricant to the correct level on the dip-stick. You have to allow a few moments for any fresh oil you've added to drain down into the sump to get an accurate reading.

RUBBER BELTS

Now look at the rubber belts as we outlined on page 97, checking the slack in the longest section of the belts and examining them for damage or fraying. The workshop manual will suggest intervals at which you should automatically exchange them, and you should make sure you get the correct replacement. Adjust the belt tension by slackening the generator bolts as we described earlier, and replace the belt according to the workshop manual's instructions if the recommended service interval has elapsed or if you find signs of damage. The place to look for the latter is on the underside of the belt, where its surface actually contacts the pulleys. You may find it to be cracked, brittle, oil-soaked, frayed or torn. There shouldn't be more than about a centimetre of give in it — if there's more, then the belt tension needs to be adjusted according to the instructions in the manual. This usually involves slackening the pivot bolts on the generator so that the whole unit can be pulled further out to a position where the belt is tighter, then pulling up the pivot bolts again without letting it slip back. You will need to prise the generator outwards with a large screwdriver to keep the belt tight while you fasten the bolts. Aim for a half-inch or so of slack on the longest run — if you pull it up so tight that you could play the harp on it, you'll be placing extra wear on the generator and water-pump bearings and they'll let you down sooner or later.

Some cars are equipped with a single large belt driving a number of accessories. These belts have a **tensioner** mechanism to keep them taut, and you have to lever the tensioner back by locating the point of a large screwdriver behind some protruding part of the engine block and pushing the shaft against the tensioner until the belt is loose. This system is not adjustable — the tensioner automatically applies the right pressure to the belt.

ADJUSTING THE FAN BELT

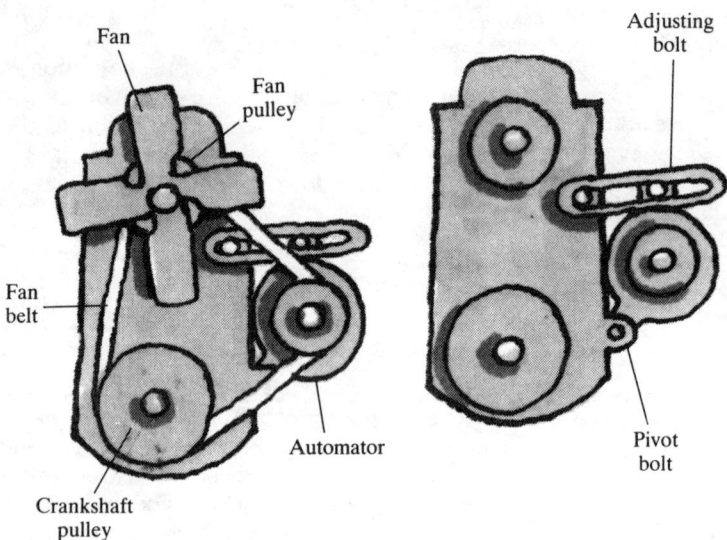

Fan

Fan pulley

Fan belt

Crankshaft pulley

Automator

Adjusting bolt

Pivot bolt

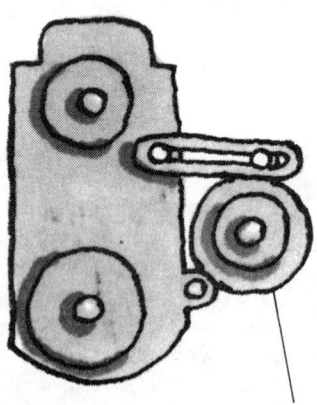

When pivot and adjuster bolts are slackened off, automator can be pivoted to adjust play in fan belt

Crankcase ventilation. A variety of systems designed to vent fumes from the interior of the engine and prevent the build-up of sludge is used on modern cars. Some emission-control or 'anti-smog' valves require periodic cleaning and examination, and the workshop manual will advise you as to what type of device you have.

IGNITION

The most important things to remember at the outset about the ignition system are:

★ **Have your replacement parts** to hand if you think you're likely to be renewing the contact points. New points are a cheap service item and have too critical a role in the car's performance to be worth penny-pinching over.

★ **Take a note** of the order in which the bits came apart.

★ **Be very careful** not to drop any of the small nuts and screws that hold ignition parts together into the murky depths of the engine. Not only is this the kind of event that can swiftly trigger hysteria, but if you drop such a thing into a place from which you can't retrieve it — such as the choke tube of the carburettor for instance — you could wreck your engine into the bargain. In all these manoeuvres, **take your time**. Don't contemplate these jobs, at least the first time you explore them, if the deadline for getting the car roadworthy again is two hours away.

However, the only tools you'll need for this adjustment and/or examination are a screwdriver, a feeler gauge, a 'points file' and a set of tiny ignition spanners or a small adjustable wrench, all of which the accessory shop will furnish you with once you tell them what you're doing. And for distributor lubrication — and lubrication of many other small fittings on the car, and in the home for that matter — a small trigger-operated oilcan is invaluable. Fill it with ordinary engine oil and squirt a *sparing* quantity into whatever you're directing it at when you squeeze the handle. Control of the supply of lubrication is vital with distributors. If you slop a lot of oil in, the car will rebuff this kind of attention by failing to start.

Check that the car's ignition is turned off. Then take off the distributor cap as you did in the examination in the last chapter. Then remove the rotor arm as you did before. In some distributors there is a plastic shield between the rotor and the contact points. This simply lifts off.

Once again, refer to your manual for a description of the specific

117

maintenance your distributor needs. Some are fitted with a felt 'wick' in the top of the spindle where the rotor sits, and this should have a few drops of engine oil applied to it. The automatic-advance mechanism (the system of centrifugal weights we described in Chapter Two) should be lubricated with a few drops of engine oil squirted through the aperture in the baseplate under the points. Put a *very small* smear of grease on the cam face that bears on the moving contact of the points. Some sets of replacement points are supplied with a small quantity of grease included.

As we described in the keeping-tabs-on-your-garage section, you should now inspect the inside of the distributor cap for signs of carbon tracking, corrosion of the contacts or weakness of the central contact that bears on the top of the rotor. If the cap seems in a bad state, or there are signs of tracking, scrap it. Replacement of the cap is straightforward enough, but since it does involve removing all the sparking plug leads and fitting them to the new one, **make a note of which sparking plug each ignition lead goes to before you pull it out of the cap**, otherwise you'll get in a fearsome tangle afterwards. Most distributor caps these days have simple push-fittings for the ignition leads, but some older ones have a 'lid' on the cap that has to be unscrewed, and the leads are pressed on to spikes underneath. Even if you aren't replacing the distributor cap, it's a good idea to check inside the connections where the plug leads push into their terminals, because if neglected these areas can become picturesque displays of green corrosion, a highly non-conductive substance that needs to be cleaned out with a wire brush.

Now examine the **contact-breaker points**. Cleaning and adjusting the points is really the first job you can do on your car that enters into the realm of the moderately skilled, rather than simply the rudimentary, the inconvenient or the downright filthy. However, when you've done it once it never seems so threatening again, particularly if you've improved the car's performance, often to a surprising degree.

Disconnect the small wires passing from both the condenser — the small, cylindrical object — and the moving contact of the points. They will normally be secured with a very small nut, hence the need for the set of small spanners or the little adjustable one. The condenser is usually secured to the distributor separately and won't need to be removed unless you suspect trouble with it — about which more later. Note that some cars now have renewable points/condenser packages that are replaced all of a piece.

REPLACING THE CONTACT POINTS

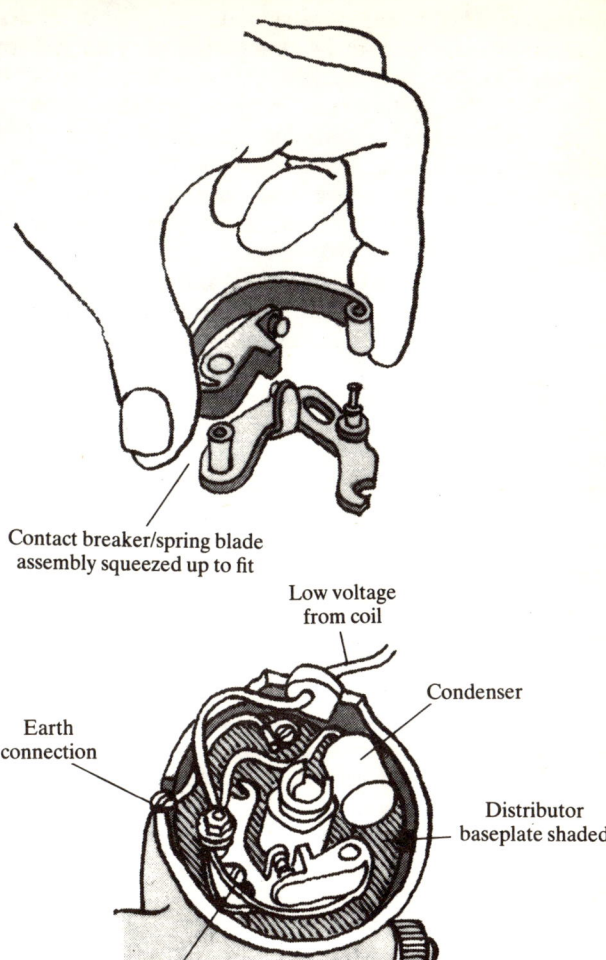

Contact breaker/spring blade
assembly squeezed up to fit

Low voltage
from coil

Condenser

Earth
connection

Distributor
baseplate shaded

Locking screw

Distributor with cap
removed showing
contact set installed

The points themselves will be secured to the baseplate by one or two screws. If the car is old, and if it has been ham-fistedly serviced, you may well find that a succession of mechanics or do-it-yourselfers have knackered the screws by persisting with the wrong-sized screwdrivers. If you use a tool that's too small for the job you will certainly do this. If the screws are poor, replace them at this service. Once they have been removed and put carefully aside, you can then lift the moving (spring-blade) contact off its spindle, and take out the fixed contact that sits on the baseplate after it.

Look closely at the faces of the points. They are likely to be blackened slightly, but they shouldn't be excessively burned, and they should be free of oil or grease. You can clean them up by carefully rubbing the faces with the points file, taking care to rub off the little 'pip' that always grows on one side — though of course you won't be able to get rid of the corresponding dent created in its opposite number. The workshop manuals will usually say you can get away with this cleaning-up operation once, so you will need to replace the points every other time you do it. We would tend to recommend rather that you replace the points with new ones at *every* service, since they're cheap and so crucial to the car's well-being. And if you discover very severe burning of the points — possibly accompanied by backfiring when the car is in use — replace the condenser at the same time, an equally straightforward and inexpensive job.

Either way, replace the points the way you took them apart, (in reverse order), but leave the adjusting screw — the one that fastens the fixed contact to the baseplate through an elongated hole in the former — loose for the time being. These days contact points are manufactured with the part that passes over the pivot pin on the baseplate already made of an insulating material. On some older cars, the moving contact is all metal, and there's an insulating sleeve and a complicated arrangement of washers that keeps the contact electrically separate from the pin and the baseplate. If you have this type, take extra special care on dismantling that you make a note of the order in which everything goes back. But the principle to bear in mind is that current must not pass between the moving contact and its pivot pin. If it does, the engine won't run.

Now you need to set the distributor spindle up so that the points are in the position they would be in if a cylinder — usually number one cylinder — was just firing. As we explained before, the gap between the contact points at this stage is crucial to how the engine behaves. Arriving at the correct position can be done in a variety of ways. Now that most engines don't have a crank-handle, you can't use this to rotate it, but if it's a manual-gearbox car, put it in top gear and have somebody push it slowly (double-check that the ignition is *off*) until you see the distributor spindle turn to the point where the moulded 'heel' of the moving contact is sitting right on the apex of one of its raised cams. This is the points' fully-open position, the one at which the gap adjustment is performed. Your assistant will, incidentally, be less likely to have to visit the nearest out-patients' for hernia treatment if you first remove the sparking plugs according to the instructions further down. This removes the compression from the engine and means there's a lot less resistance to push against. If the car's an automatic, you can't push it in gear, but you can have an assistant briefly flick the starter key on and off to 'bump' the engine round on the starter motor until the cam is in the appropriate position. And if you want to get flash about it and you don't mind the investment, some accessory shops will quite cheaply sell you a device called a **remote starter switch**, which you can wire up to the engine and use like a starter key under the bonnet, and with which you can effect much finer degrees of crankshaft rotation as well.

Check the points gap in the manual. Then sort through the blades of your feeler gauge until you find the one (or a combination of two) that corresponds to this measurement. Put the gauge squarely between the contact points and move the lower 'fixed' contact under its adjusting screw until the points just nip the gauge. Then tighten up the securing screw and measure the gap again. Some-times the act of tightening the screw slightly tightens the points gap as well and you need to slacken it off and do it again. Consequently you may find that starting the tightening operation while the gap is still a little slack results in the measurement being just right once the screw is tightened fully home. Some distributor designs make all this easier by having automatic adjusters that vary the size of the gap as you turn a screw on the contact. The manual will warn you if you are to expect this.

It's worth noting that manuals increasingly specify a measure-ment by **dwell meter** instead of by feeler gauge. This is not as horrendously complicated as it sounds. The dwell meter is just an electrical test-meter that measures what proportion of the 360° swept by the rotating distributor spindle actually involves the points being closed (the **dwell angle**), a measurement naturally made while the engine is running. Dwell meters can be bought cheaply at accessory shops, often as part of more elaborate test-rigs that will also perform other useful tasks, and full instructions are supplied with them. The actual manipulation of the distributor points after you've made the measurement is almost always identical to what we've described above, though some General Motors cars have a 'window cap' distributor, on which you can adjust the dwell angle while the engine is actually running. Once again, the manual will advise.

IGNITION TIMING

By now, you should have a fairly clear idea about what the ignition timing means and why it's important. The spark has to light the fuel in the right cylinder, and at the right position of the valves and piston to impart the maximum push to the piston to provide power. Its timing also has to be slightly varied to take in a range of driving conditions and loads.

There are now sophisticated methods of checking the timing electronically, but there are also basic checks you can perform yourself. Because they involve removing the distributor cap and the rotor arm, it makes sense to do them as part of your general servicing of the distributor. But make sure you do a timing check *after* you've attended to the points. Points renewal slightly alters the ignition timing and you may need to adjust it afterwards.

The first thing to note is that the position of the distributor body can be varied in relation to the spindle that runs through the centre of it, as we discussed earlier. Alterations to the position of the points in relation to the spindle and the cams that flick the points open and shut can be done internally — by centrifugal weights in the base of the distributor that slightly move the baseplate — or externally, by the suction of a vacuum device linked to the carburettor that can rotate the entire distributor body. Furthermore, you can alter the position of the body yourself and thus alter the starting points of these operations. Below the distributor body, just at the point where the shaft disappears into the engine, there will be a clamp bolt and nut, like a kind of handcuff around the shaft. Alternatively there will be a flat plate sitting beneath the distributor, with a bolt passing straight through it into the engine. Slackening either bolt will allow the entire distributor body to be turned. The rotor arm inside the distributor is likely to be marked with an arrow indicating its direction of rotation, so turning the distributor in the *opposite* direction will *advance* the ignition — that is, make the spark happen earlier — and turning it the *same* way will *retard* it.

You now need the manual again. The car's makers will specify a figure, in degrees, for the ignition advance — in other words, at how many degrees before the position of absolute maximum lift of number one piston (**top dead centre**) the contact-breaker points should open and provide the spark. Don't worry, you don't then require a protractor and an evening class in geometry to figure out when the engine is actually at this position. The makers help by providing markings both on a rotating part of the engine — usually the flywheel rim or the crankshaft pulley driving the fan belt — and on some fixed part adjacent to it. The manual will tell you where these markings are, but if you haven't already cleaned the engine you may have to do a bit of judicious scrubbing to uncover them. Then you do your pushing-the-car-in-top-gear routine, or manipulations of the starter motor, to turn the engine to a position where the rotating mark and the stationary mark line up.

Now inspect the contact points. The apex of one of the cams on the distributor spindle should be just about beginning to push the points open. If the timing is out, slacken the clamping bolt under the distributor and gently turn the body until the points are about to open, making sure that the position of the markings on the engine hasn't changed. The best method of establishing the 'just-opening' position is to enlist the help of a test-lamp from an accessory shop — a screwdriver-like object with a light in its handle and a lead with a clip on the end. Secure the clip on to the small electrical terminal on the side of the distributor (the one you had to disconnect to remove the points) and wedge the sharp end against some metal part of the engine, or the battery earth terminal itself. When the points are closed, the light will be out, but the instant they begin to open, the light will come on. Obviously this is a better way of finding precisely the right position than screwing your eyes up to try to establish whether the points have opened by the thickness of a gnat's whisker or not. Once you're satisfied that the distributor body is in the right position, retighten the clamp bolts, and the 'static timing' will be correct.

There are a couple of other checks you can make on the ignition system before you put everything back together. Remember that we have several times described the mechanisms the car needs to advance and retard the ignition timing according to usage. There is a **vacuum**-operated device, connected to the inlet manifold on the cylinder head, which varies the timing according to the load on the engine. The speed at which the engine can revolve is not simply a function of how far your boot has descended on the accelerator pedal. You might have the pedal almost on the floor but a heavily loaded car could still be ascending a steep hill in third gear with the engine revolving quite slowly. Conversely, the accelerator might be only slightly depressed while you're driving a lightly loaded car on a level road quite fast in top gear. The vacuum advance is sensitive to these changes and alters the timing accordingly.

To check that it hasn't failed, rotate the baseplate of the distributor mechanism against the resistance of its spring and hold it there. Then pinch the small tube you will find running from the inlet manifold beneath the carburettor to the miniature cymbal-like device (the vacuum unit) attached to the side of the distributor. Release the baseplate, and although it will move slightly back towards its original position, it won't slip all the way back unless the unit is leaking. If it seems OK, stop pinching the tube. The plate should now return to its original position. If it does this only slowly, or not at all, then its return spring is binding. In the case of either fault, the vacuum unit should be replaced. You should either visit your service station to get this done, or establish the details for your car from the workshop manual.

To check the mechanical or **centrifugal** advance, refit the rotor arm to the distributor spindle and twist the whole lot clockwise. When you release it, it should spring sharply back to its original position. If it doesn't, the centrifugal advance may be faulty and your service station should take the matter further. In any event, if there is serious wear on the centrifugal mechanism, it may well make sense to have the distributor unit replaced in its entirety.

Lastly, an appendix to the subject of ignition timing. There are other ways of timing the ignition that take into account the full range of the distributor's activities. For instance, you can observe whether the advancing and retarding of the timing is happening when it should, by connecting a neon or xenon light into the sparking-plug circuit, highlighting the fixed and rotating timing marks with a strip of white paint on each, and then running the engine with the flashing light playing on the marks.

This performance has a stroboscopic effect, whereby the marks appear to be stationary. The reason is that the timing light will flash only when number one plug is firing, and it should do this only when the two timing marks are actually passing each other. You can adjust the position of the distributor until they're exactly in line. You will also see them move as the advance/retard mechanism operates when you accelerate the engine. High-street accessory shops sell cheap timing lights, and they come complete with instructions. But the static timing method is quite adequate for normal servicing, since you'd be wise to take the car somewhere with electronic diagnostic equipment for a double check once a year anyway.

While you're on the ignition, check the sparking-plug leads for signs of perishing or chafing. It's a wise precaution to replace your sparking-plug leads every 30,000 miles or three years, or at the outset of your ownership of the car if they look fairly well-travelled and you don't know when they were last changed. Get a ready-to-fit replacement set for your model from the agents or an accessory shop. This pack has all the end-fittings already in place. So all you have to do is pull each lead from the distributor cap — they're generally a push-fit — and from the sparking-plug cap, and replace each with one of a corresponding length from your new set.

Change them one at a time, so you don't lose track of what goes where. Most modern ignition leads have a built-in suppressor to stop the ignition interfering with radio waves, and these leads should be used exactly as supplied and not cut to fit, or they won't work.

SPARKING PLUGS

These are the parts of an engine that almost everyone is familiar with. They're also regarded as something of a password to instant engine repair, since people experiencing misfires and malfunctions always blame the plugs and replace them whether they have any bearing on the problem or not.

It's certainly true to say that the condition of the plugs is vital to proper performance, and an inspection of them also provides some useful clues as to what the condition of the engine actually is. Label your plug leads with masking tape before you remove them so you know what order to reassemble them in.

Start by pulling off the plug cap with its attendant lead — do this gently, and pull on the cap, not the lead. Then fit your **sparking-plug spanner** securely over the body of the plug, and unscrew it. Sometimes plugs will be in quite awkward positions, tucked behind generators or squeezed next to distributors, so that it's difficult to get the plug spanner lined up. The type of spanner with a universally jointed socket is useful here. In a really difficult case where you might need the universal joint but also the plug is buried quite deep between components, you might have to resort to buying a separate plug socket, universal joint and long socket-bar to get to it.

Once you have all the plugs out, examine them to see what clues you can get about the condition and adjustment of your engine. Remember that the electrodes of a sparking plug are the curved metal strip — which is actually an extension of the threaded portion (the 'outer electrode') — and the 'central electrode', which runs vertically through the plug. The gap between these two is critical. Signs and meanings include the following:

★ **Normal plug** — both electrodes should be clean, light-brown or tan in colour, and unworn — in other words, there shouldn't be a small 'bite' out of the electrodes at the point where the spark jumps between them. A plug in the latter condition can be cleaned, regapped and reinstalled.

★ **Overheated plug** — wear is likely to be present in a plug that has been overheating. The colour will probably be off-white, and the tip of the insulator — inside the plug and surrounding the central electrode — may be cracked or breaking up. A plug in this condition should be scrapped. Check the serial number on it with the car's agents to establish whether it was actually one of the wrong heat range for the engine in the first place. There are other causes of plugs overheating — wrong ignition timing, wrong carburettor adjustment, or fuel of too low a star-rating (octane value) for the engine.

★ **Sooty plug** — dry, soot-like deposits on the electrodes are caused by the fuel mixture being too rich, by the ignition timing being out, or possibly by recent cold-weather short-haul driving during which the choke has been operated a lot. Plugs in this condition can be cleaned, regapped and reinstalled, but the cause of the soot needs to be discovered and put right.

★ **Oily plug** — quite distinct from the sooty type. If there is oil on the plug tip, still wet, then the stuff is getting into the combustion chamber by a route that you will need to establish. You can, once again, clean and reuse plugs suffering from this condition, but it's only a temporary remedy.

★ **Damaged plugs** — possibly exhibiting electrodes burned away, insulators cracked away from the central electrode and other horrors. An insulator crack may be the result of clumsy gap-setting, but the other conditions are all the result of premature ignition or overheating. Scrap the plugs and find the cause.

If you're going to put your old plugs back to work, you need to know the correct cleaning method. The simplest recourse is to get a local service station to clean them on an abrasive sand-blasting machine designed for the job. You can, however, make a reasonable go of it yourself. Start by attacking them with some engine-cleaning solvent on a cloth, to get the body and threaded section as clean as you can. Then get hold of a **wire brush** and scrub the inner part of the plug with it — between the electrodes, and between the central electrode and the inner walls. Use the ignition-points file to bring both electrodes to a shiny condition.

Then check the plug gap in the works manual. You can set this by using your feeler gauge and bending **only the outer electrode** until the gap is correct. It's better, however, to use a round-wire type of gap gauge specifically intended for plugs, which the accessory shop will be able to provide. This device is also likely to include a gapping tool, which will bend the electrode without damaging it.

ADJUSTING THE SPARK PLUG GAP

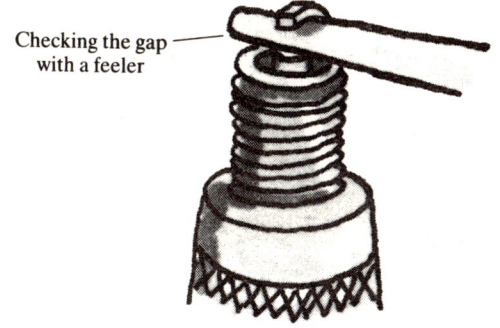

Checking the gap
with a feeler

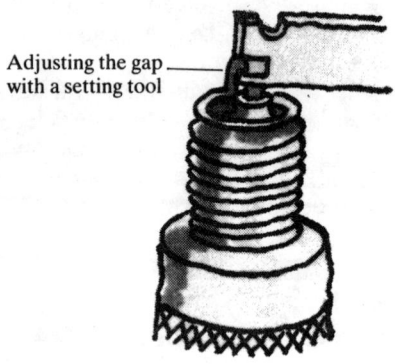

Adjusting the gap
with a setting tool

Replace the plugs by screwing them in by hand until they're finger tight. It's tempting just to shove them into the end of the plug spanner and rotate them with the handle, but there are nasty risks attached to doing this. If you don't get the plug started off straight in its thread, the extra leverage you get from using the tool might mean that you tighten it in cross-threaded — particularly on an aluminium cylinder head. If this happens, you're in all sorts of trouble and will need professional help to get your head sorted out, as it were. There is *no risk* of this happening if you feel the plug in by hand. Once the plug has gone in as far as it will with only your finger to propel it, use the spanner to give it a final pull-up. But don't shift the spanner more than half a turn beyond the position where the plug is fully finger tight, or you may strip the threads. Once again, aluminium cylinder heads are the most vulnerable to this mistreatment.

AIR FILTER

This is straightforward enough to replace. The manual will once again specify the frequency — it could be at service intervals of 5000 or 6000 miles, half that distance in exceptionally dusty climates, or double it in damp ones. Flat, pancake-like filter housings are usually installed over the air intake to the carburettor, and these covers are generally secured by one or more fasteners (either nuts or screw-headed ones). You remove this — or these — and lift the cover off, revealing the air-cleaner element. While you're at this point, be doubly careful that you don't drop any small metal objects down the exposed centre, because it leads straight into the carburettor and from there to the combustion chambers and you'll never get the offending articles out again without taking the engine to pieces. Replacement of the paper-element filter is simply a matter of getting hold of the right service part, making sure it's the right way up, dropping it in and refastening the lid. Some **oil-bath** types have a wire-mesh filter instead, which you don't throw away. Take it out, wash it in paraffin, let it dry, then douse it with engine oil to trap any dust, and replace it.

SEASONAL SERVICING

There are some considerations that don't necessarily fall in with the regular service intervals but which you need to do before drastic changes in temperature, i.e. in the spring and in the autumn.

Start by repeating all the basic cooling-system checks we described on page 87. Then you need to descale and flush out the water system in anticipation of the kind of conditions that may cause overheating. This is an operation that in Britain is conducted more in hope than in expectation, but in some parts of the world it can make all the difference between agreeable and infuriating motoring.

Start by draining your cooling system down, following the manual's instructions as to the whereabouts of the taps. Refill with clean water and add a proprietary descaling compound from an accessory shop — the accompanying instructions will tell you how long you are recommended to run the engine for after introducing it. When that period has elapsed, drain it off again, flush the system through with cold water to wash out the additive (this is particularly recommended for the reservoir of a sealed cooling system), and then refill with the standard mixture of water and antifreeze.

Whilst attending to the cooling system it makes sense to check the thermostat as well. It's normally fitted at the junction between the upper radiator-to-engine hose and cylinder head and should be renewed every two years. You can test the thermostat by removing it according to the manual's dismantling routine, submerging it in a saucepan of water and bringing it slowly to the boil — shortly before the water boils, the circular valve on the thermostat should open. If it opens when the water is lukewarm, or is open all the time the thermostat is out of action, then the effect it will have on the car is to prolong the warm-up time unduly and make the heater ineffective. If it never opens, even when the water boils, then it will already have been causing severe overheating in your engine. Replace it.

THE ENGINE — MECHANICAL CHECKS

We're not at this stage assuming that you're desperately anxious to start tearing your engine apart. Replacing the points and checking the timing might already have seemed to you to be operations fraught with complexities. But there are some basic mechanical checks including 'adjusting the tappets' (that famous phrase always invoked whenever a joke conversation about car expertise is embarked on) that are no more involved than replacing the points and which are essential to combat the slow deterioration caused by wear and tear.

Firstly, remember what we said at the start about getting things clean. The use of a proprietary engine-cleaner, brushed or sprayed over the engine — with the carburettor, distributor and plug leads protected by plastic bags — and then hosed off with water will make all these operations easier and much more agreeable to perform.

Now some checks to stop things from falling off. With the engine warm but not so hot that you can't touch it, check over the nuts and bolts that hold the manifolds (the castings on to which the carburettor and the exhaust pipe are mounted) to the cylinder head. Leaks here will upset the running of the car (particularly at idling speed) and all the nuts should be good and tight. Make sure that the nuts holding the carburettor to the inlet manifold aren't slack either, but don't twang so many muscles in the effort to get them really tight that you distort the flange of the carburettor and make things worse. Incidentally, you may well find that your **ring spanners** come in really useful during these operations. Open-ended spanners are notoriously hard to fit into the little niches between the manifold castings in which the retaining nuts are prone to skulking. Sockets would be even better.

Don't attempt to tighten or alter nuts on the *top* of the cylinder head, if any are visible around the edges of the oblong rocker-box cover on top of the engine. That's because these nuts will be the ones that hold the cylinder head to the block — and both the order in which they've been tightened and the precise degree of effort involved in tightening them are critical to a degree that might surprise you.

Before you go any further, make sure you've acquainted yourself with information as to whether your car is equipped with **overhead cams**. Chapter Two will have told you what to look for. An **ohc** (overhead camshaft) engine is one in which the camshaft (or camshafts) is mounted above the valves and knocks them open and shut directly. This type of engine is much harder to adjust the valve clearance on. Check the manual's recommendations, but if you feel faint-hearted entrust the job to a specialist.

Conventional **push-rod** engines, with the cams mounted lower in the crankcase and operating the valves by rods and levers (**rockers**), are much more common and much simpler to service.

If this is the type you have, you can move on to the valve-clearance adjustment. If the manual recommends doing this with the engine hot — and this is by far the most common practice — then run it again for 15 minutes or so, or take the car for a short drive until it's back at its normal operating temperature. Now remove the rocker-box cover.

Normally there will be two nuts securing it to the head, and it will be sitting on a cork gasket which may well tear to shreds when you lift the box off, in which case a replacement will be necessary — all accessory shops stock them for popular cars. Underneath you'll see an imposing array of springs and strange, baleful-looking lumps of metal.

If you remember our observations in Chapter Two about the operation of the valves, what you're actually looking at are the push-rods coming up from the camshaft, the see-saw rockers that are pushed up at one end by the rising rods and thus descend at the other end to push the valves open, and the coil springs that snap the valves shut after each one has done its job in the cycle. The gap between the end of the rocker and the stem of the valve when the valve is fully closed is crucial to engine performance. If the gap doesn't exist or is too tight, the expansion of all the metal parts when the engine gets really hot means that the valve never fully closes properly — which reduces the compression of the engine and prevents the valve from dissipating its heat into the head. The result is that the car runs badly, and the valve overheats and eventually burns out.

The phrase 'adjusting the tappets', though this is the one most frequently hurled around, is actually technically incorrect. The tappets are inoffensive little items — which at our level of intrusion into the innards of the engine you'll never need to confront. They actually sit between the lower ends of the push-rods and the camshaft. What you're really going to adjust is the **rocker clearance**. Find out what this measurement should be from the car's manual. There will often be a figure for the inlet valves and a figure for the exhausts, a recommendation as to whether you should perform the operation with the engine cold or hot, and a little diagram showing you which is which and in what order the adjustments should be made. The latter sequence is important, because it enables you to be sure that each valve is fully closed when you carry out the adjustment — an operation that will require the same old tedious performance of putting the car in gear and pushing it about that you had to do during the points-gap service.

If you're in doubt about where each valve should be when you attend to it, the following rule of thumb is reasonably accurate: turn the engine over until the valve about to be adjusted closes — in other words until its push-rod appears to have descended to its lowest point or the valve spring is fully expanded. Turn the engine *slightly* beyond this point and you won't be far out.

Then you'll need your feeler gauge again, a screwdriver, and a spanner (preferably a ring spanner) that fits the nut you will normally find on the 'back end' of each rocker, immediately above the push-rod. This is by far the most common arrangement, though some engines have eschewed rockers all pivoting on the same shaft and have them pivoting on separate studs — the manual will specify what sort of attention they should get.

Check the tappet clearance when each valve is fully shut by pushing the feeler-gauge blade of the right dimensions between the valve stem (the bit protruding through the centre of each valve spring) and the end of the rocker arm. If it won't go in, the gap is too tight, and it's too loose if you don't feel the 'pull' of the rocker on the feeler as you slide it in and out. In any conditions other than perfect, slacken the nut above the push-rod on the rocker you're adjusting, and — stopping the nut from further rotating by keeping the spanner on it — screw the adjustable ball in and out with the screwdriver until the gap measured by the feeler is right. Keep the ball from rotating by maintaining pressure on the screwdriver, simultaneously pulling up the nut to lock it.

Do this all the way along the valve train, either following the method recommended in the manual (which will often prescribe a sequence in which the full opening of one valve is taken as an indicator of the full closure of another) or using the closed-valve-plus-half-a-turn method we described above.

Once you're satisfied about this, replace the rocker box — renewing the gasket if necessary — and tighten down its retaining nuts.

FUEL SUPPLY

It's impossible to overestimate the importance of being systematic in the checking and servicing of motor cars. It's relatively easy to appear heroic in the emergency circumstances of fixing a break-down, or to get a great deal of smug satisfaction out of repairing a *major* breakdown. But the more boring routine of following a regimen when you service the car rather than just doing the bits you fancy can prevent you from having the breakdowns in the first place.

This is why it's important to ensure that all kinds of other problems — air leaks at the manifolds, inaccurate valve-rocker clearances, wrong ignition timing — are sorted out first before you move on to the fuel system. Otherwise you can end up making adjustments to everything at the same time, and the poor car ends up sick in every organ rather than just the one that was originally making it suffer.

Modern **carburettors** are complicated instruments, maybe the most advanced combination of delicate engineering and complexity of parts apart from the electronic computers many machines are fitted with these days. As a consequence, over-optimistic or ignorant attention to them can cause all manner of havoc. Also, modern engineering is increasingly developing more and more efficient alternatives to the carburettor in the form of fuel injection — a system more complicated still. Basic servicing is therefore best restricted to cleaning and possibly diagnosis of faults, which a specialist will be required to correct. Remember before we proceed any further that **petrol is dangerous. Don't explore any part of the fuel system with a naked light nearby, and avoid working in such a restricted space that a build-up of fumes can occur**.

Start your service of a conventional fuel system at the **fuel pump**, and at the appropriate section in your workshop manual. The pump may be electrically or mechanically operated. If it's the latter, you'll certainly find it mounted on the crankcase somewhere, and either type of pump will be identifiable through the sleuth-like operation of tracing the flexible petrol-feed pipe from the carburettor to wherever it leads in the engine bay. A mechanical pump has a gauze filter fitted beneath a domed metal or perspex cowling, and you can remove the retaining screw on top of it, lift off the cover, take out the filter and clean it with petrol. Be careful when replacing the cover that its gasket is fitted correctly, and that the fibre washer is present under the retaining screw. Air leaks into the pump reduce its efficiency or can stop it completely.

On an electric pump, the filter will normally be in the union where the fuel pipe from the tank joins the pump, and the union will need to be loosened with an adjustable or open-ended spanner.

Fuel pumps are always available over the counter for popular cars, and replacement of them is a straightforward job. The manual will advise, but in the case of a mechanical pump driven off the engine's camshaft, it's important to ensure that the gasket where the pump is bolted on is undamaged or replaced with a new one.

CARBURETTORS

Carburettors have grown dauntingly sophisticated. Remind your-self of the principle (see page 27). The pumping pistons suck air into the engine through a carburettor, which is a rabbit-warren of tiny airways and fuel passages. The air passing through in turn sucks precisely-metered quantities of fuel — the metering achieved by means of the predetermined sizes of the passageways — from a reservoir on the carburettor. That in itself is basic enough, but modern instruments have jets and passageways for idling, for pro-gressive acceleration, for sudden acceleration, for cold running (some with automatic thermostatically-operated chokes), and for high-speed cruising. If you take such a thing apart and reassemble it with even one jet replaced somewhere it shouldn't be, the car will let you know it in no uncertain manner. Even alteration of the linkage that connects the accelerator to the choke mechanism can cause havoc if you don't appreciate the precision with which it's been set up.

Caution is therefore mandatory, however smart you think you are. Whatever you're intending, check the details with the work-shop manual first. You will also need to remove the air-cleaner assembly from the top of the carburettor — generally by first taking its top cover off as you did to change the element, at which point it will either lift off or there will be further fasteners in the bottom of it, and probably some form of external mounting to the engine as well. You can service the **filter** first of all — unscrewing the nut-like union that joins the fuel intake from the pump to the carburettor body, and behind this, or integral with it, will be a gauze filter which you should blow clean.

Then prepare to service the **float chamber** by either removing its upper cover — normally retained by screws — or lowering the chamber from the instrument. Be careful when you do this, because you will be disturbing the float which is delicately set and could be skewed by ham-fisted dismantling. You are then likely to find a certain amount of sediment in the bowl, which you should flush out with petrol, making sure that you don't propel it back into the fuel ducts in the base of the chamber. Check the float itself, and remove the needle-valve assembly, which can be unscrewed with a small spanner. If you find there is a ridge rather than a smooth and even surface on the little conical 'needle' that the float bears on to, renew the needle-valve assembly complete, and make sure you don't omit any of the washers that sit underneath it.

The workshop manual will also tell you about the position of the **jets**. Symptoms of jet-blockage are 'flat spots' during acceleration, stalling or hard starting that your attention to all the other engine ancillaries has not been able to improve. On some carburettors jets can be straightforwardly removed for cleaning with a spanner or a screwdriver, but they should be **blown through** only, *not poked with wire or needles*. Attacking them with such implements can alter the delicate machining and upset the fuel flow. In other designs they can be got at only by the carburettor body being taken apart, which is best done with the instrument off the car and also best left to a service station.

If your car has a **variable-choke** carburettor then the procedure is slightly different. This is a design that is at least blessed with simplicity, since there isn't the usual labyrinth of channels and jets but a single jet — the size of which can be constantly varied according to what the engine and your accelerator foot are up to. The fuel mixture is simply being sucked through a fine tube containing a long needle in it which is fine at one end and slightly thicker at the base. The needle fits into a piston that also sits in the engine's air intake. The speed at which the air is being pulled in varies the height of the piston, so the size of the fuel-intake tube is varied according to how much of the tapered needle is 'obstructing' it. This kind of jet is almost impossible to block, but you do have to service the float chamber and needle valve as above. And as we described in the last chapter, you need to unscrew the piston damper from the top of the carrburettor and make sure there's engine oil in it. You can't actually overfill it, because reinserting the damper and screwing it back forces excess oil out through a pin-hole in the top.

TOPPING UP S.U. AND STROMBERG CARBURETTORS

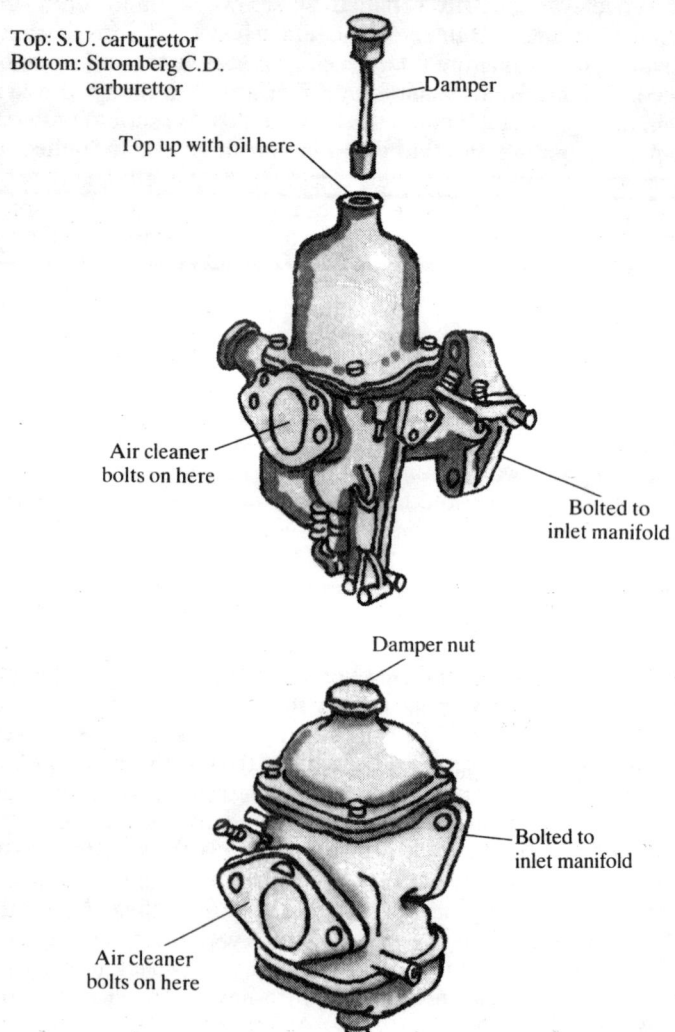

Top: S.U. carburettor
Bottom: Stromberg C.D. carburettor

Damper

Top up with oil here

Air cleaner bolts on here

Bolted to inlet manifold

Damper nut

Bolted to inlet manifold

Air cleaner bolts on here

Don't forget to check any **in-line** filters your fuel system may have. You're likely to find such a thing in the pipeline between the pump and the carburettor in the form of a small metal or plastic canister with filter-paper inside. Cars with fuel-injection systems instead of carburettors sometimes have these filters fitted near the fuel tank instead, which the manual will tell you about. Either way, these are not serviceable. You simply remove the filter by unscrewing the hose clamps, discard it and fit another at the service intervals. Note the arrow indicating the direction of fuel flow — the filter isn't meant to be fitted either way round. And carefully follow the manual's instructions in the case of an injection system. Fuel pressure in these systems can be very high, and you need to know how to relieve it if you aren't to spray fuel everywhere when you start dismantling.

ADJUSTMENT

Fixed-jet carburettors have traditionally had two adjustment screws to establish the correct idling speed. One is the **throttle stop**, which establishes the position of the butterfly valve between the carburettor and the inlet manifold (see page 27) when the engine is idling. The other is the **mixture control**, which alters the proportion of petrol to air. The standard method of adjustment of such an arrangement is to get the engine thoroughly hot — carburettor adjustment is pointless on a cold or lukewarm engine — and then set the throttle-stop screw to give a steady tick-over. You can find the throttle stop, because it's the screw close to the carburettor body against which the throttle comes to rest when you release the accelerator. You could get an assistant to do this while you look closely at the instrument. The manual will then tell you where the mixture-control screw is, and you slowly move this in and out with a small screwdriver until you get an exhaust note that is as even as possible. Doing this may have quickened the idling speed, in which case you can slow it down again at the throttle stop. That's all there is to it.

Recently manufacturers have been sealing the mixture screws, as we pointed out earlier, because they don't want random amateur adjustment leading to breaches of the pollution laws in some countries. Carburettors of this type are meant to be set up with the aid of an electro-chemical exhaust-gas analyser, and you shouldn't mess with them. Some late-model vehicles are fitted with computer-controlled idling, and these are not amenable to adjustments either. Last in the list of restrictions imposed by modern engineering is the idling mechanism controlled by an electrical solenoid. This is designed either to control the tendency of the engine to run on after the ignition is turned off, or to raise the idle when power-consuming accessories such as air-conditioning are on. Adjustments to the latter should strictly follow the manual's recommendations.

On the **variable-jet** type of carburettor, the throttle stop is much the same as on the fixed-jet, but you can alter the mixture by raising or lowering the jet assembly in relation to the tapered needle. You can do this by using a spanner on the nut at the base of the instrument below the jet — screwing the nut upwards weakens the mixture by reducing the gap between the needle and the jet, while screwing it downwards enriches it. Check the manual for any special instructions regarding the choke-operating levers while this operation is going on.

Lastly, **multiple** carburettors. Most basic and family cars don't have more than one, but sportier models do and the synchronization between them is crucial. The best advice we can offer on adjusting them is: don't. Their mixtures and the amount of air they draw in have to be precisely established, and getting these cockeyed can be the kind of operation you wish you'd never started because you can never get back to where you began. Leave it to a specialist with proper tuning equipment unless you're *very* enthusiastic — in which case it will entail studying the makers' instructions carefully, and investing in some of the DIY air-speed balancing equipment sold by rally and accessory shops.

FUEL INJECTION, DIESEL POWER AND TURBO-CHARGERS

Of the three systems listed above, the first and the last were for many years treated as the special preserve of the race-track, and the second as that of the farmyard, the building site and the haulage industry. Now all three are finding their way into quite ordinary road transport. This has come to present special problems for the do-it-yourselfer — and some of them are insuperable.

Fuel-injection systems, as we outlined in Chapter Two, depend on squirting the correct fuel-air mixture direct into the cylinders without the maze-like construction of carburettors, and micro-technology has further advanced the accuracy with which the mixture can be established and adjusted to driving needs. From the consumer's point of view this can result in better starting, better all-round performance, increased economy and reduction of pollution, because there are sensors relaying data to the computer from the exhaust, the throttle mechanism, temperature gauges and so on. Some injection systems use a device that externally is rather similar to a carburettor (**throttle body injection**), others have an injector supplying each cylinder separately (**multi-point** or **port injection**).

The principal departure from the carburettor is that the injection system forces fuel into the engine under *external* pressure, rather than relying on the suction from the pistons to get it to where it should be. The injection system therefore uses a high-pressure pump, often mounted near the fuel tank, and a complex system of engine sensors and, latterly, computers to work out how much fuel and air is needed. If you get a problem with a fuel-injection system that isn't solved by a change of the air filter and the fuel filter, go to an expert. On a computer-controlled system, the mechanic needs to put the computer into its self-diagnostic mode to get clues to the malfunction (often failure of one of the sensors) and then be able to interpret what they mean. Leave injection systems alone.

Diesel engines are not yet in widespread use in standard motor cars, but several makers now offer a diesel car as part of their range. The efficiency of a diesel engine is higher, so you get better fuel mileage and this is why British cab-drivers use them. They can run on leaner mixtures, they cause less pollution and they work by piston-compression of air to raise its temperature so that it spontaneously ignites the fuel. They don't need an ignition system either.

However, they tend to be noisier and sometimes harder to start in the cold, they need more frequent oil changes, and diesel fuel is prone to water contamination. On a diesel engine, your foot on the accelerator is not altering the rate of air flow, but controlling the spray of fuel from an injection pump, a device that administers high-pressure fuel to the engine in precisely-timed pulses. Such requirements as giving the fuel more time to burn at higher speeds — the function of ignition timing in a petrol engine — are met by the pump 'advancing' its injection timing.

Once again you can't do much servicing to a diesel system, particularly to the injection pump which requires meticulous skills in rebuilding it. You can, however, adjust the idling speed by turning a screw that is a part of the throttle linkage, as it is on a petrol engine. Refer to the workshop manual for the details of your particular model.

Turbo-charging, a brutal performance-enhancer that has been used in competitive motoring for some time, has recently come into more general use on standard cars. It's simply a method of forcing in more air under pressure than the engine would suck in of its own accord. Maintenance of turbo-chargers simply falls within general lubrication attention, except that the makers may specify more frequent engine-oil changes because the speed at which the bearings of the 'blower' spin puts a big strain on them. After an oil-change you will probably be asked by the owner's handbook or the manual to spin the engine on the starter with the ignition disconnected (with the lead from the coil to the distributor pulled out of the cap and grounded on some part of the engine's metalwork, *away* from the fuel fittings) so that the turbo-charger's oil supply can prime itself before getting going in earnest.

Trouble with turbo-chargers is mostly restricted to noisy operation when their bearings wear out or faults in the **waste gate**, which controls the flow of exhaust gases through the turbine and prevents it from running too fast. Once again, the manual for your type of charger will explain the layout. Armed with such information, you can inspect the waste gate while the car is revved up to see if it's functioning properly.

TRANSMISSION

Compared with the performance you can go through to keep the engine running sweetly, the transmission requires little routine attention beyond ensuring that gearboxes and final drives are properly lubricated and that clutch adjustments — where there is scope for adjustment — are taken care of.

Starting with the latter, the **clutch** needs the kind of routine attention we outlined on page 101 when we were covering the checks you could make on work carried out by your garage. In that section we dealt with the clearance that needs to be maintained on many cars, which you experience as a small amount of slack at the top of the clutch-pedal travel before meeting the resistance of the springs and which is, in fact, a measured amount of play at the release lever on the clutch housing itself.

Not all cars have this arrangement. The adjustment is designed to compensate for wear on the clutch plates, but some clutches are self-adjusting, and the manual will inform you if this is the case. If you have a **hydraulically-operated** clutch — in other words, one in which your pressure on the pedal moves hydraulic fluid down a pipeline to a small piston that activates the clutch — then you will need to locate the master-cylinder reservoir and check that it holds the appropriate level of hydraulic fluid. If it doesn't, it needs to be topped up. You may be able to use a good-quality universal fluid for this, or the makers may specify one type in particular. If the level is seriously low then there's probably a leak somewhere, which is most likely to be visible as a seepage of oily liquid at the cylinder end, close to the clutch-release mechanism. If this is happening the cylinder will need to be dismantled or replaced. If you leave it you will shortly find yourself with no clutch action at all, which is severely incapacitating.

MECHANICAL CLUTCH ADJUSTMENT

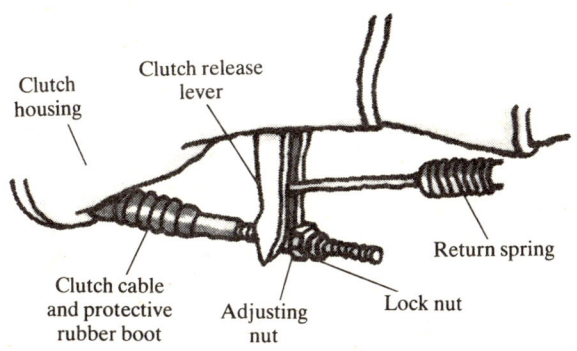

HYDRAULIC CLUTCH ADJUSTMENT

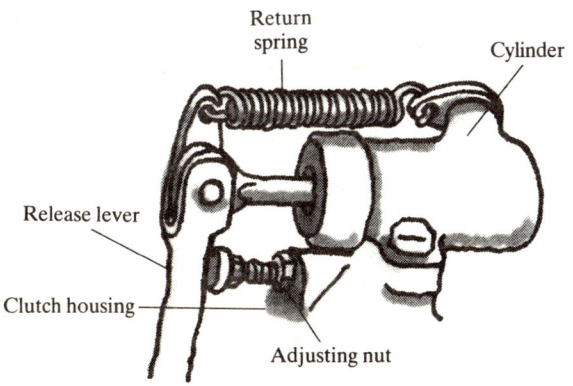

As a cheaper alternative to renewal, the piston can be removed from the cylinder and only the rubber seal on the barrel replaced. But make sure:

★ That the piston barrel isn't scored, scratched or worn.

★ That you keep everything scrupulously clean, and dip the new rubber seal in clean hydraulic fluid before you reassemble it all.

★ That after rebuilding the system you refill it at the reservoir with *fresh* fluid and not with the stuff that came out when you took it apart.

★ That you open the bleed valve on the cylinder slightly and use the pedal to pump any air-polluted fluid out before you retighten the valve and set off.

The cleanest and most effective way of doing this is to fit a sutably-sized clear plastic tube to the **bleed valve** and discharge the fluid into a jar. Accessory shops sell bleed kits for attending to both clutches and brakes. The plastic tube has the added advantage that you can see any air bubbles in the line as the fluid emerges, and you should continue to pump it and replenish the reservoir until no more bubbles appear. All hydraulic systems need to have any air bubbles 'bled' out before they're fully efficient. Bear in mind that hydraulic fluid is fearsomely corrosive stuff, particularly to car paintwork.

The nature of hydraulic clutch systems is such that they take up wear in the plates of their own accord, but on a rod or cable system there is likely to be provision for adjusting the clutch, and the manual will specify the dimensions of the clearance. The likely method will involve the loosening of a **locknut** on a threaded section of the operating cable or rod, pulling the latter into such a position that the specified clearance is recovered, and then retightening the locknut in the new position. If you have a transverse-engined car, the adjusting bits and pieces are likely to be under the bonnet, but on an in-line, rear-drive car they will probably be underneath. Use ramps or axle stands for safety if you can't reach the mechanism by squeezing under without lifting the vehicle.

GEARBOX

Whatever kind of gearbox your car is fitted with, its innards should forever remain a mystery to you, unless you develop a messianic zeal for taking cars apart and you have a lot of time on your hands.

The only maintenance needed by any gearbox — automatic or manual — is for you to ensure that its lubricant is at the correct level. Some gearboxes, particularly automatics, have a dip-stick as the engine does, and the use of this is straightforward. In other designs, the filler plug also acts as the level gauge. In other words, once the oil overflows the orifice, you know you've got enough. Make sure that you put the filler plug back securely and that its washers are undamaged. And top up the gearbox with whatever oil the makers recommend. This is important, because transmission oils are not the same as engine oils and you can damage a very expensive piece of equipment by using the wrong type.

The gearbox should never need to be more than slightly topped up, however. If you have to keep doing it then there's a leak probably at the bearings at one or other end of the unit and this will need to be fixed if a mishap is not eventually to befall you. Complete replacement of the gearbox oil is nowadays very rarely called for, but the makers' recommendations should be followed. And when you're topping up a gearbox or an automatic transmission, **don't let dirt or grit get in,** and take care that you clean all loose dirt away from the filler plug before you take it out. Gears are hard-wearing things, but gravel in the works reduces their longevity no end.

The same rules apply to the **rear axle** if your car is of the type in which the final drive and the gearbox are housed in separate units. And if your car is fitted with an **overdrive**, consult the manual for any observations about adjustment of the **lock-out cable**. Neither overdrives nor rear axles are really amenable to home maintenance and if you experience trouble with either, take it to a specialist.

TRANSMISSION JOINTS

We covered on page 74 the checks you need to make on transmission joints — the things that transfer the drive to the roadwheels. In the past, they were always fitted with grease points that needed regular attention from a grease gun, but sealed-for-life joints have virtually banished the need for such an implement. Check in the manual if these components need any regular attention.

Either way, at each service you should continue to check for wear in the joints, and for any damage to the rubber gaiters that protect the joints and retain the grease. If there are any grease points — shafts that telescope into each other on grooved 'splines' sometimes feature them — make sure you invest in a small grease gun and attend to them. This needs to be done however hard to reach they are, because awkwardly-placed lubrication jobs may well have been neglected by previous owners and the result is always a failed component in the end.

STEERING GEAR AND HUBS

Once again, the tendency over the past twenty years or so towards the use of plastics and sealed joints has virtually eliminated any requirements for lubrication servicing of the steering parts, but if there are any the manual will tell you so.

Like hubs, the steering parts are grease-packed on assembly and sometimes it is a service operation to dismantle them, wash out the grease with solvent and repack with fresh grease. This is done because the lubricating qualities of the grease deteriorate over time owing to the high temperatures caused by the spinning wheels. It can also be the case that adjustment of the hubs is called for. This is a more complicated operation, sometimes calling for special extracting tools to pull the hubs off and a **torque wrench** for precisely measuring the tightness of the hub nut — in which case our advice would be to leave it to the service station. If you do your own services, don't let the difficulty of this job persuade you to neglect it or tell yourself you'll leave it 'for later'. Your life could depend on it.

If you have **power steering** there will be a reservoir of hydraulic fluid, as there is for the brakes and clutch. The system is sealed, however, and if you find the level dropping, go to an expert to find out why.

Carry out the general steering and suspension checks we ran through on page 102. It may be necessary to effect some kind of adjustment on both steering gearboxes and rack-and-pinion systems, in which case it will involve taking up wear by altering the relationship of the moving parts. The manual will describe any such manipulation, for which the first step will normally be raising the front wheels off the ground and securing the car. Then set the roadwheel in an exactly straight-ahead position. If you have a steering gearbox, slacken the locknut and turn the adjusting screw until it hits a solid object (the rocker arm), then turn the wheels slowly through their full arc to ensure that they don't bind at full locks but there is a slight 'tight spot' in the centre position.

Then tighten the locknut without letting the adjusting screw move any more. **Rack-and-pinion** boxes need more complicated treatment, since you have to add or subtract very thin pieces of steel **(shims)** between the rack housing and its cover. If you feel this is too momentous a task but your earlier tests on the steering (see page 104) have revealed wear in the rack, don't whatever you do neglect going to the service station to sort it out. Rack adjustment, if it's feasible on your car, will nevertheless be fully explained in the workshop manual.

SPRINGS AND SHOCK ABSORBERS

These parts are also virtually maintenance-free nowadays, but that doesn't cut out the need for periodic inspection. Check what maintenance the makers require. If there are grease points, grease them. If you have **leaf springs** — several thin strips of steel bound together — they may require squirting with lubricant, unless they are interleaved with rubber or plastic in which case external lubrication will ruin them, so make sure you know which type yours are. And if you do have to use oil on the springs, don't get it on to the brake apparatus or on to any of the rubber linings (**bushes**) that the springs or shock-absorbers pivot on.

Very old-fashioned lever-type shock-absorbers need to be topped up with a special fluid but modern telescopics are sealed and can be replaced only when they start to shed their contents.

Examine the suspension thoroughly for loose nuts and bolts, torn or perishing rubber parts, broken springs and signs of wear or slackness where there are arms joining the axle parts to the body-work. Dismantling of the suspension is a formidable and potentially dangerous job for a home mechanic because the compression that coil springs are under can make them hazardous once you release the tension. Leaf springs, however, can be more easily removed and repaired according to the makers' instructions. However, the nuts and bolts holding them are likely to be hard to shift because of road-dirt and corrosion, and a thorough soaking in penetrating oil is invariably a sensible preparation.

If you fear suspension trouble, don't ignore it but get the garage to attend to it if you can't. Anything that upsets the handling characteristics of the car makes it dangerous to drive, and faults in these areas will prevent it from getting a roadworthiness certificate anyway.

WHEELS AND TYRES

Unless the manufacturer specifically recommends otherwise, it's a good idea to swap the wheels and tyres around at the service intervals to spread the wear. You do this by loosening the wheel nuts with the wheelbrace while the car is still on the ground. Trying to undo a wheel nut once the wheel's lifted and can spin freely is the sort of operation that only trying to plug a mains-water leak with you finger can rival in futility. The wheel nuts may be behind a **hub-cap** which might need removal by being levered off at the rim, or by the extraction of a retaining bolt. The nuts are likely to be pretty tight. Wheel-nut removal — and replacement — is one of the areas of motor maintenance that those who doubt the capacity of their forearms and wrists may balk at. If you're going to need muscular help, call it up before you start on this operation. You can get added leverage to loosen a stubborn nut by extending the wrench with a length of metal pipe but *don't* use this to tighten the bolts up again.

Swap the wheels diagonally corner-to-corner, or the fronts with rears on the same sides. Tighten the nuts up again as hard as you can with the wheelbrace, but don't impose excessive force such as by putting your foot on the brace because you may strip the threads or start cracks in the wheels. The wheel nuts, incidentally, are usually domed — with the curved part nestling in a hollow in the wheel. Make sure you put them back this way round.

Examine the tyres during this operation for splits, cracks, bulges, or penetration by nails or glass. Check the wheel rims too, and don't forget the spare. You may find that the car has at some time hit the kerb, with the result that the wheel rim has buckled, possibly causing a bulge in the tyre. If you're doubtful, go to the garage for a second opinion. Uneven wear on the tyre — even as severe as baldness on one part and normal tread on another — is a sign of wrong inflation or of faults in the suspension or steering set-up of the car. More wear in the centre of the tyre than at the edges is a sign that it has been running underinflated for a long time. Measure the treads with a tread-gauge, available from accessory shops.

If the depth of the tread — in other words, the distance from the top to the bottom of the 'grooves' — is less than 1 mm, replace the tyre. You can get a replacement either at the service station, or from a specialist tyre-supplier where you may get a better deal — which you should be able to find through recommendation or the local trade directory. The specialist will remove your old tyre, fit the new one to your wheel, inflate it and, if you wish, remove the wheel from the car and replace it while you wait.

At the service intervals, get the garage or the tyre specialist to check your wheel balance on the special equipment they have for the job, and adjust the weights if necessary.

BRAKES

When you read in the motoring press of doubts being expressed by the manufacturers (and sometimes by the motoring organizations and the police) about home servicing, the reliability of the attention being given to the steering, suspension and brakes is often the major reservation.

The first point to make is that if you experience any abnormality in the working of your brakes — squealing, swerving, long pedal-travel before anything happens, or if you have to pump the pedal to slow the car, or falling fluid-levels and visible leaks from any of the components — you should fix it or have it fixed **at once**. A slight brake squeak in wet weather is common on some designs, but metallic scrapings or shriekings are not. The second point is that though all of the stages of your routine service are vital, many of them are vital principally to save you inconvenience and unnecessary wear on your car. Servicing of the running gear and the brakes, however, is vital for quite another reason — your life and that of others.

Brake testing is something that only service stations are equipped to carry out properly, because they have special meters designed to measure the effort. But you can get a rough idea of the efficiency of your system on a straight and unoccupied stretch of road. Begin by driving the car at only 10-15 mph, and apply the brakes hard once you're sure there is no following traffic. If this test is OK and the car does not swerve or fail to respond properly, then perform a proper measured check. You will need to establish some marker as the point of reference, accelerate the car to 30 mph and hold it at that speed until you reach the marker, then apply the brakes hard. If the distance from the point where you braked to the point where you finally stopped is 30-35 feet, the efficiency of your system is good. If it's 50 feet it's fair only, and if it's much higher than that it's distinctly poor.

Routine maintenance of the brakes is restricted to keeping the fluid-level in the reservoir topped up (this should in any event be a weekly examination), examining the linings or pads for wear, and carrying out adjustments if the design permits it.

The only tool you may need for adjustment is a **brake-adjusting spanner**. Ordinary spanners can be pressed into service, but use of the right tool prevents rounding of the edges of the adjuster which can make subsequent maintenance a nightmare. If you have disc brakes all round, this is all an irrelevance because they're self-adjusting and the only maintenance required is changing the friction pads. Some adjustable brakes need screwdrivers rather than spanners, and some drum brakes have self-adjusting mechanisms. You may have a mixture of brakes, with discs at the front and drums at the rear.

Adjustment to drum brakes involves raising the wheel in question off the ground until you can spin it. Locate the adjuster or adjusters. Some will be on the back of the brake-drum (the **brake backplate**) in the form of one or two hexagonal-headed fittings, and others will be reached through a hole in the wheel — the manual will tell you where to look. If they're on the backplate, clean the dirt off first. Then fit your brake spanner on the adjuster, tighten it clockwise until the wheel locks solid. Slacken it back gradually until the wheel is just free to spin again. If there are two adjusters, do one at a time. If you're doing a rear brake, make sure that the handbrake is off before you attempt adjustment.

The handbrake system is adjusted separately. Because it usually operates through cables running from the lever to the brakes, adjustment takes the form of compensating for the stretching of the cables in use, because the effects of wear on the shoes will already have been taken care of in the operations we just described. If you find that when you pull the handbrake full on, the car still isn't properly anchored, the cables need adjustment. Ideally the handbrake shouldn't need to be pulled more than three or four notches to be fully applied. Check the manual for the specifics, but the principle — rather similar to that of mechanical-clutch adjustment — involves simply slackening locknuts on the cable and screwing up the adjusting nuts secured by them until you start to feel the brake shoes retarding the spin of each rear wheel. Then slacken the nuts just enough to free the wheels again and pull up the locknuts to stop them shifting.

While you're on the handbrake mechanism, examine the cables for fraying, wear or jamming. If they look dodgy, or if the stretch is so great that no more scope for adjustment is available, renew the cables.

You won't need to replace **brake pads** or **linings** at each service interval unless your driving habits are appalling, but it's wise to examine them and make a note of how fast wear is progressing. As usual, read your workshop manual first to figure out your car's particular needs for this job. Replacement of disc-brake pads is straightforward enough, but removal of drums can sometimes call for special extractors, and if this is necessary you might want to leave it to someone else.

The regular procedure for drum brakes is as follows: loosen the wheel nuts on the brake you're starting at, jack up the car and remove the roadwheel. Then ascertain how the drum is secured, slacken off the brake adjustment completely, remove the fasteners and pull the drum away. You will almost certainly find dust inside it. You need to get rid of this. Do it by rubbing the inside of the drum with a solvent-soaked rag to mop it up rather than by blowing it out, then throw the rag away — the dust may contain asbestos and you shouldn't get it in your lungs. The brake shoes will be revealed, and you can assess their condition. The thickness of the lining shouldn't be less than $\frac{1}{16}$ inch at any point, and the linings should be free of contamination by oil or grease, which will look like highly polished dark patches. Once again, you can clean dust from the backplate and around the hydraulic cylinder or cylinders with the rag.

If you've concluded that the shoes need replacement, remove any retaining clips they have and then prise one shoe out of its slot in the wheel cylinder — it just fits in there, it isn't fastened — with a screwdriver at one end, and ease it out of the slot at its other end. It should now be possible to wangle both shoes, complete with their 'pull-off springs', away from the backplate. Before you take every-thing apart, make a mental note or a sketch of the positions of any springs, exactly where springs of different lengths are meant to go, and what holes they hook on to. Wind a tough elastic band around the pistons protruding from each end of the wheel cylinder or cylinders, and then test that they're free by pushing each piston gently in turn and ensuring that the movement pushes out the one at the other end. Don't let them come right out of the cylinders though, or you'll get a fluid leak and have to bleed the hydraulics down. While you're inspecting the brakes, make sure there are no leaks from the cylinders anyway, give the entire area a thorough clean and lubricate the adjusters if they're stiff.

Replace the brake shoes with identical ones, and make sure you get manufacturers' recommended spares because inferior copies may give you inferior brakes if the stuff the linings are made of isn't up to scratch. If you have self-adjusting shoes, then the adjusters will be mounted on them and will have to be transferred from the old set to the new. The suppliers of the shoes may well do this for you. How you replace the shoes depends on the layout. It may be best where there are long springs running from one shoe to the other, to lay out the whole arrangement off the car, carefully pick it up complete and then locate one shoe in its slots in the cylinders and lever the other one over with the screwdriver. Some designs may suggest fitting one shoe with its springs and then attaching the other to it. Consult the manual for advice.

If the condition of the hydraulic mechanism isn't in doubt, you can now put everything back. Make sure that whatever you've done on one side of the car you do on the other side as well, or the braking effort may be uneven. Check also that the shoes are level with each other and are fitted centrally on the backplate, and that the adjusters are fully retracted or you won't be able to get the drum back on. Refit the drum and retighten whatever was used to retain it. Readjust the brakes as we described earlier and you're ready to go.

In the case of **disc brakes** the procedure is a bit different. Attend to one wheel at a time — you'll find it easier to make an examination if the roadwheel is removed. After that, you'll see the disc — which should be polished, and free from corrosion and deep score-marks — and the jaw-like calliper which 'bites' on it. Bearing directly on either side of the disc are the **disc pads**, which are the renewable part. You should replace them if their thickness is down to between $\frac{1}{16}$ in and $\frac{1}{8}$ inch — different makes will have different tolerances. Spring clips or retaining plates or bolts may have to be removed — the manual is the guide. It will also explain the need to push the hydraulic pistons in as far as possible when replacing the pads. Keep everything clean and, as with regular brake shoes, don't put greasy fingers on the friction material. It will never work properly if you do.

If your car happens to have disc brakes all round, then the adjustment of the handbrake will be different — and some versions will be self-adjusting. Since the usual arrangement is one whereby there is a separate pair of pads at each rear wheel for the handbrake, these will also have to be maintained according to the makers' specifications and replaced when the friction faces are excessively thin.

If you did discover leaks, or if the handling of the car has suggested hydraulics problems — in the form of weak braking when the linings or pads are otherwise good, a spongy brake pedal that needs pumping, or swerving when the brakes are applied — then you may conclude at this point that you want the specialist to take it from here. This would certainly be our advice if you really are new to car servicing. If you do feel confident about going on, however, we can provide a rough outline of the steps you have to take.

Start by establishing the correct **hydraulic fluid** for the system if you don't already know this. Then locate the **bleed valves** or **nipples** on each brake. These are the means whereby the system can be drained if all the fluid is going to be renewed, and whereby air can be bled from it when everything is back together.

If your examination has revealed a leaky wheel cylinder on a drum brake, remove the drum and the shoes, put a newspaper under the hub, take off the rubber end-covers from the cylinder and *gently* push out the pistons, which will probably emerge complete with a retinue of springs and flat washers. Make a note of the order in which all these parts go. Some fluid will also come out with them, so get someone to keep the reservoir topped up or you'll draw air into the system at the supply end and have to bleed the brakes all round. Examine the barrels of the pistons in a good light, and shine a light into the bore of the cylinder which doesn't have to be removed from its location. If you can see obvious wear and scuffing, or signs of trapped grit scoring the walls, then scrap the entire cylinder by unscrewing the hose from behind it and removing the bolts that hold it to the plate, and renew it with a factory replacement.

If the barrels and bore look OK, buy the appropriate wheel-cylinder service kit from the agents or a good accessory shop and carefully fit the new parts to the pistons. Wheel-cylinder rubber seals are conical and must be refitted only one way round — look at the originals and the drawings in your workshop manual for guidance. Before carefully reassembling, clean all the metal cylinder parts and moisten all the rubber parts in clean brake fluid — **never** use anything else to clean brake components.

You will then need to **bleed** the brakes. Kits are available from the accessory shops that enable you to do this single-handed, and some even cleverly make use of the air pressure from your spare tyre to force the fluid in without pedal pumping. If you don't have these tools, then this is the method at each wheel. Ensure that the level in the reservoir is where it should be and that you have plenty of fresh fluid to hand. **Thoroughly clean** the bleed nipple, push a clear plastic tube on to it and submerge the other end in a jam-jar with some fluid already in it. Unscrew the bleed nipple half a turn and have your assistant pump the brake pedal to force fluid through. Some systems require slow depression of the pedal and quick withdrawal, some a slow movement in both directions, some a kind of quick-quick-slow — the manual will again be helpful. When air bubbles have stopped emerging form the tube, tighten the nipple again while the pedal is still being held down. Make sure that you're keeping the reservoir topped up all the time this business is going on.

The same operation can be done at the **master cylinder** if there are leaks from there, but if your car has any pressure-limiting valves or skid-control systems, you should have the operation of these checked by the specialist. Servicing of the seals in disc-brake callipers requires the removal of the calliper from the car, but beyond that the servicing of the rubber parts is similar to that for the regular wheel cylinders. And if you have servo-assisted brakes which the manual will inform you of, replace the rubber components in the servo at the same time as you perform a general brake overhaul. The servo's air filter and the lubrication of its piston may require attention as well.

Lastly, if you find yourself doing an all-round brake overhaul and you've therefore drawn in air at all four wheels or are completely replacing the fluid, start your final bleeding operation at the nipple furthest away from the master cylinder and work towards it.

UNDERBODY ATTENTION

While you're performing this scrutiny of those dirty and out-of-the-way parts of the car, you have to keep an eye open at the same time for the ravages of rust. This can not only ruin the value of your car but make it dangerous to drive as well. As you examine the suspension and the brakes, check also the points where the suspension mountings are fitted to the bodywork, and the engine and transmission mountings. Check the metal brake pipes for rust that might lead to fractures and leaks, and look for holes or weak spots in the floor-pan, the seat-belt anchorage points, the jacking points and the box sections under the doors.

Check also pages 174 to 176 in the final chapter. If you discover an absence of underseal, surface rust beginning to get a hold, or substantial build-ups of mud in obscure corners inside the wings and around the backs of the light fittings, now is the time to organize that visit to the steamcleaners and follow it with some form of rustproofing treatment.

ELECTRICS

And finally to the nervous system of the car which, you'll be relieved to learn, doesn't need much routine attention.

You already know about checking the battery's fluid-level and keeping it topped up with distilled water, and about ensuring that the terminal clamps on the battery posts are tight and clean. You can take the battery off the car to charge it, and when you do this you should loosen the cover or stoppers to release any pressure during charging.

Make sure you connect the charger's leads to the battery the right way round or you'll discharge it instead and be worse off than when you started. And if you find that your battery has got to the stage where charging it results in only limited improvement, get the garage to do a high-rate discharge test. This may reveal that the battery is on its last legs. Replace it with one of the right type for your car, and fit its terminals the right way round. You may find that if you buy one from an accessory shop you have to add its electrolyte yourself. Usually this will mean the battery can be used immediately, but for preference it should be given a short boosting charge first.

Your check on the rubber belts will have already established whether failure of the charging circuit through belt breakage is imminent. The generator or alternator and the charging-regulator mechanism are not open to home maintenance, though the dynamos fitted to older cars can sometimes have their carbon brushes examined — you can do this by removing the cover over the brush gear and ensuring that the small black blocks bearing on the polished copper drum (the **commutator**) haven't dwindled to less than ⅛ inch in length. More recent dynamos have to be taken off the car and the two long bolts passing through them unscrewed before you can take the brush cover off.

Replacing brushes can be the sort of simple-looking operation that results in visits from the men in white coats, because of course they're vigorously sprung against the commutator and you've got to be able to hold them all back before you can slide it in again. If you do get this far, clean the commutator with a rag very sparingly damped with solvent. Burning or wear on the commutator, or signs of burning anywhere else in the dynamo mean you should take it to an auto-electrician for examination.

The same goes for the **starter motor**, which is constructed very similarly to the dynamo but is usually blighted by its positioning low on the engine block and by the fact that it is frequently obstructed by other ancillaries. The manual may specify regular starter maintenance in the form of light lubrication of the end of its central shaft, but that's all you can do. If your car develops sluggish starter action and you can absolve the battery and the battery-to-starter connections from blame, you may be able to get as far as removing it — which usually involves undoing two or three highly inaccessible bolts — and possibly even replacing worn brushes. Further electrical work on it, however, should be left to the expert.

Alternators, which have largely replaced dynamos, should not be dismantled. But you can easily remove one from the car if you're experiencing a charging fault, and take it to an auto-electrician for repair or exchange.

No other maintenance of the electrics is necessary beyond checking that all the lights and dashboard instruments function and replacing any blown bulbs with the correct spares. It also makes sense to cast an eye over as much of the wiring loom as you can see, to ensure that cables have not worked loose from their clips and are not in danger of chafing through against exposed metal. Keep an eye on the condition of your windscreen-wiper blades — if they fray or become ineffective replace them at once — and ensure that the horn and the screen-washers work. Internal failure of these items will need specialist help or replacement, but before you opt for either of these, check the condition of the terminals where they receive their electricity supply and where they're earthed to the body. Corrosion or dirt on cable junctions and earths can put any electrical device out of action.

8

ENTROPY

'Things fall apart; the centre cannot hold'
(W. B. Yeats)

'I think he's stopped breathing. What do I do now?'
(James Thurber cartoon on artificial respiration)

At some point in your motoring life your car will break down. There may be, somewhere, a motorist who has clocked up a substantial mileage and never had this happen to them, but we doubt it and we have never encountered such an individual ourselves. The complexity of the motor car, the economics of building an average vehicle to a price, human error, the speed at which its moving parts relate to one another, the ravages of the elements and the diseases its raw materials are prone to all conspire to maximize the likelihood that one day you will come to an involuntary stop.

One precaution you can take in this lottery is to join the kind of motoring organization that will come out to help you, come day or night, rain or shine, winter or summer, and will possibly arrange to ferry you home or wherever you're headed if they can't get you going themselves.

Even if you know something about the workings of the motor car, it makes sense to enlist in such an organization. Representatives of the good ones come out to you fully equipped, highly experienced, and, what's more, willing to try to solve your problem whatever the hour and the weather when lying under the car yourself is the furthest thing from your mind — even if you knew what was wrong anyway.

But when mishaps occur, it helps to know which ones are simple — and therefore amenable to fixing in the time it would have taken to locate a working call-box and wait for the cavalry — and which ones oblige you simply to hope that getting towed home will be the least of your expenses. We therefore now abandon you to our spot-the-bug analysis of what can go wrong, why, and what you can do about it, incorporating a brief run-down of quick roadside checks and get-you-home repairs.

Your tools for this kind of rudimentary fault-checking will have to include a **pair of pliers with insulated handles**, a **sparking-plug spanner**, **spanners to fit the fuel-system unions**, a **feeler gauge** and a small quantity of **insulated wire** — like the stuff you'd buy for wiring in accessories like extra lights. We would also strongly recommend that you always carry on the car a **spare set of points**, a **spare condenser** and a **spare set of sparking plugs**. None of these items is expensive, and having them with you could get you out of a hole when you least want to be in one.

A final piece of preparatory advice would be that when it comes to trying to sort out a roadside breakdown while your loved ones watch despairingly from behind the windscreen, it can save much time and misery if you already have a rough idea of how the ignition, carburation, starter and battery systems work. Getting to know your car for the first time in a hailstorm, looking for a blocked petrol filter when you don't know what the carburettor is, is a daft way of going about it.

BREAKDOWNS

A) Engine does not start and the starter motor will not spin it — i.e. turning the key produces only a sluggish rotating sound or a dull click.

Causes: Battery discharged, loose battery terminals, faulty starter, jammed starter pinion, faulty ignition switch, seized engine (unlikely).

Checks: Turn on the headlamps. If they're *dim* or the light is non-existent, the battery is discharged or the terminals are loose or dirty. Check the latter, clean and retighten them if necessary. If there is no change, you will have to bump-start the car (getting someone to push you, preferably down a slope, while you turn the ignition on and bring up the clutch pedal smartly with the car in third gear) or, if it's an automatic and you can't do this, borrow some electricity from somebody else's battery via jump-leads. Be very careful to link the positive pole of one battery to the positive of the other, and the negative to the negative, and make sure the jumper clamps are firmly attached to the terminals. If the car starts, go straight home or to a garage (be careful not to stall) and get your battery recharged. Remember you can also *tow-start* a car by the same method as the bump, but don't crash into the back of your saviour.

If the lights are *bright*, however, turn off the headlamps but leave the sidelights on and operate the starter again. If they now dim or go out, the trouble may still be a battery in a low state of charge, but is more likely to be a fault in the starter or its connections. Watch the ignition light on the dashboard as you operate the starter. If it goes straight out but the starter does nothing, there may be a short circuit in the starter or in the thick lead from the battery to the starter. It could also be in the solenoid, the motorized switch that will be mounted on the starter that interrupts the line from battery to starter. Check these leads and make sure that they haven't chafed through anywhere, and that no metal object is bridging their connections to the bodywork.

Clean the battery terminals if you didn't have to do this after the first test. If this makes no difference, put the car in third gear and rock it back and forth with the ignition off — if the starter pinion is jammed, this may free it. If it's freezing weather, make sure that the water pump hasn't frozen up — which it won't have done if you've attended to the antifreeze regimen we've already described. Thaw it out with a cloth soaked in boiling water around the pump's lower inlet if this unlikely event does turn out to be the problem. If, after all these efforts, the car does not now submit, resort to the bump-start or jump-lead method and examine the starter when you get home.

If the lights stay bright *while the starter key is being operated* but the engine doesn't turn, then there is current but it isn't getting to the starter. Check the terminals on the big lead from the solenoid to the starter for looseness or dirty connections, and those on the big flat braided *earthing strap* between the engine and the bodywork. If all these are OK, then the small wire from the starter to the solenoid may be loose, dirty or broken. Check this at the starter end, but at the dashboard end it may be more inaccessible. If you lose patience, revert to the bump-start or jump-leads at this point and work it out at home.

The upshot of all the above is that if your battery or your starter motor is out of action you can always still get home by the brutal methods we've described, unless the engine has actually seized — which is highly unlikely unless it's lost its oil, and anyway you'll be able to establish if this is the case by pushing the car in top gear and seeing if the resistance is abnormally high. The following faults are not always so agreeable to compromise.

B) Engine does not start but the starter spins briskly.

Causes: Now this is where we get into the realms of real motoring detective work.

When the starter motor sounds normal but the engine doesn't fire, the possible reasons are many and varied and only a systematic series of tests will crack the problem. Even with very little equipment, however, these tests can actually be performed surprisingly quickly. **Remember, however, to avoid creating sparks near the carburettor or any fuel leak.** Causes can be: damp or shorting ignition, cracked distributor parts, faulty plugs, points, ignition coil, condenser or leads, faulty ignition switch or low-tension wires, no petrol in the tank, faulty fuel pump, inoperative float-chamber needle valve or wrong float level, blocked filters or jets, vapour lock in hot weather, overuse of choke.

Before you do anything else, **make sure that you haven't run out of petrol**.

It sounds daft, but sometimes panic sets in and it's the last thing you think of — and petrol gauges can be unreliable too. Also ensure that damp or wet weather is not the cause of the problem. If there's a reason to suspect that it is, wipe all the plug leads, the distributor cap (inside and out) and the coil top with a dry rag.

If this is not the culprit, go through the following routine:

Checks: **Remove a sparking plug and lay it on any clean bare metal surface of the engine with its lead still connected**. Have someone turn the starter key to crank the engine over.

If a **'fat' spark with a sharp crack** jumps between the electrodes of the plug, you can more or less clear the ignition system of blame.

Before you leave it, however:

Lift each cap off its plug in turn and crank the engine over again, holding the cap in the insulated pliers close to the clean earth point on the engine you used to test the plug. If a spark jumps the gap from the *side* of the cap to the engine, then it's able to short to earth before it reaches the plug tip. The cap will need to be replaced, and you should bind it with insulating tape until you can get round to replacing it.

If there is **no spark at the plug**, then the ignition system needs further investigation.

Examine the plug and all its colleagues for fouling with oil, or wetting with neat petrol, which you should be able to identify by giving them a sniff. If it's the former, all you can do is clean them as we described on page 127 and later have the engine fault that is causing the problem rectified. If they're flooded with petrol, dry them off, and repeat the spark test. If there *is* a spark now, replace the plugs, spin the engine over with your foot hard down on the accelerator to dry the combustion chambers, and then try ignition again.

Continued absence of a spark needs checking back down the line.

Pull the centre lead from the top of the distributor cap, the thick one that comes from the coil to it. Hold its distributor end with the insulated pliers about ⅛ inch away from the trusty old clean earth point on the engine, and try the ignition and starter again. **If there's a spark now**, you've proved that the points, the coil and the thin wires in the ignition system (the **low-tension circuit**) are OK, so the fault must be in the distributor cap, the rotor arm or the plug leads.

TESTING THE COIL

N.B. Use insulated pliers

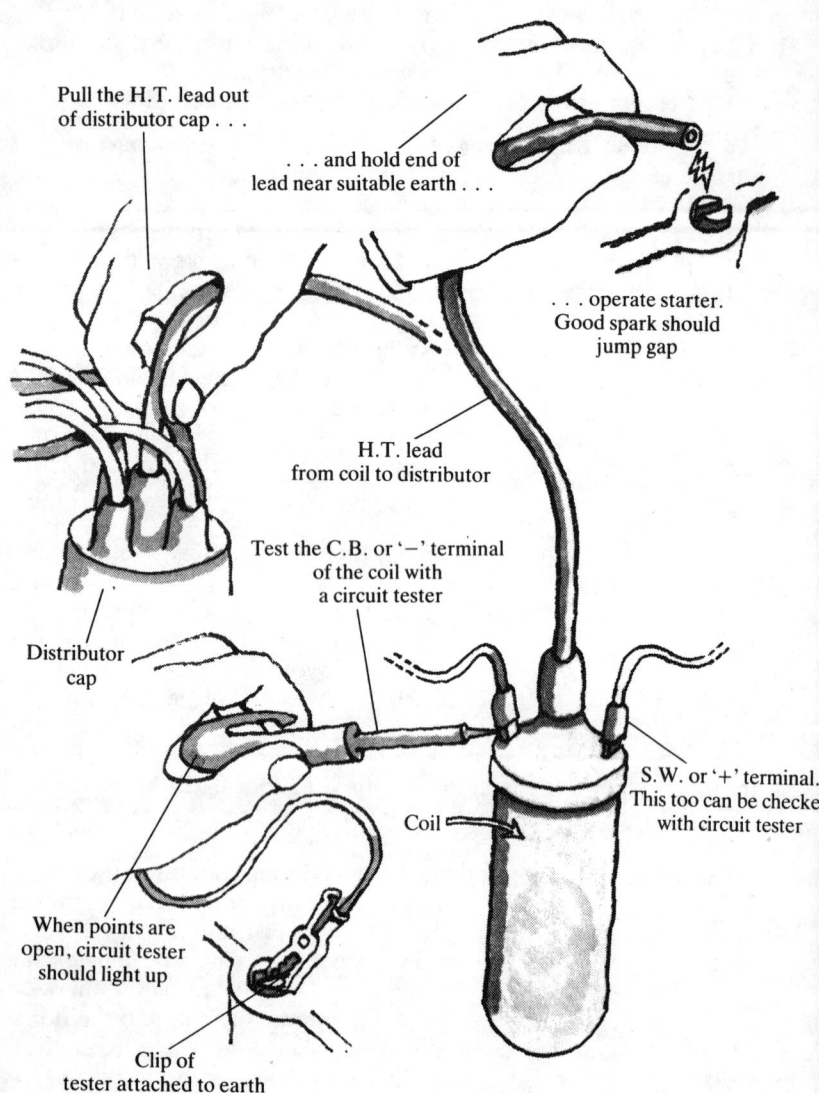

Pull the H.T. lead out
of distributor cap . . .

. . . and hold end of
lead near suitable earth . . .

. . . operate starter.
Good spark should
jump gap

H.T. lead
from coil to distributor

Test the C.B. or '−' terminal
of the coil with
a circuit tester

Distributor
cap

S.W. or '+' terminal.
This too can be checke
with circuit tester

Coil

When points are
open, circuit tester
should light up

Clip of
tester attached to earth

Examine the inside of the cap as you did in your garage-checking exercise on page 98. Bad connections where the leads fit the top of the cap, a broken sprung connection inside where current travels to the rotor, or dirt or corrosion on the rotor or the cap terminals could be the problem. Clean everything that looks as if it needs it. If the centre connection has a weak spring or the carbon brush on the end of it is worn, stretch the spring by pulling *gently* on it.

Hold the detached coil-to-distributor lead ⅛ inch from the brass section on the rotor, with the rotor in place. Crank the engine again. A spark shouldn't jump. If it does, the rotor is cracked and the spark can short to earth down it. Replacement of the rotor is the only effective answer, but if you own a popular car you might not have to go far to find a new one. However, if there was no spark when you held the distributor lead to the earth point, then the low-tension circuit may be at fault — that means the input side of the coil, the condenser or the points. The next series of tests are these:

Points test — remove the distributor cap, push the car in top gear until the points are fully closed (or turn the engine as we described earlier). Then turn the ignition on and **flick the points apart** a few times with your thumb — don't worry, this can't hurt you — and you should see a **weak spark** jump between them.

If there is no spark then check back through the ignition. **Open the points** and put a piece of card or plastic between them. Now contact a bare end of your piece of wire to the ignition coil terminal that links to the distributor — it will be marked 'CB' or with a '–' sign — turn the ignition on again, and scrape the other bare end of the wire against the clean earth point on the engine. If there's *no* spark when you do this, then either the coil isn't getting a supply, or it's damaged. If there *is* a small spark, then the blame lies either with the wiring to the points and condenser, or in a failure of those components. Let's assume the first outcome to begin with, i.e. that there is *no spark* on the test, in which case:

Disconnect the wire from the other terminal of the coil (marked 'SW' or '+') and scrape it on the earth point with the ignition on. **If there's a spark now**, the coil is faulty — there's no home-made remedy for this, and you'll have to swap it for another (virtually all motoring shops sell them). If there is **no spark** on this test, then there's no supply from the ignition switch. Get yourself home by directly connecting your spare spare piece of wire either straight from the battery — from whichever terminal is not connected straight to earth on the body — to the coil terminal from which you just removed the input wire. If the problem was only the supply of current to the coil, the car will now start, but you'll have to disconnect the wire to stop the engine, and find the faulty connection as soon as possible.

Assuming now that there is a spark on the earlier test when you shorted the 'CB' or '–' coil terminal to earth, you'll now have to check the points and condenser. Continue thus:

Disconnect the small wire on the side of the distributor, the one that links direct to the points. Scrape this on a clean earth point with the ignition on. **If it sparks** the trouble is definitely in the points or the condenser. **If it doesn't** then there's a break in this wire from the coil and you should temporarily bridge this with your piece of test-wire and locate and fix the break as soon as you can. And if you've narrowed matters down to the points, put the feed wire back and proceed as follows:

Condenser. Condenser trouble doesn't usually happen out of the blue — you generally get misfires and rough running first. If you got a **fat spark** rather than a weak one when you flicked the points apart at the beginning, then the condenser is probably shorting. Disconnect the condenser's lead from the terminal post, take your piece of card or plastic from between the points to let them close again, and repeat the flicking test with the ignition on. If the spark is **still 'fat'**, the condenser is damaged. If you had **no spark** the first time you flicked the points but get a **fat one** when you disconnect the condenser, the same thing applies. In either case, fit a replacement condenser.

If you get no spark whatever you do, this confirms trouble in the points. Examine them in the best light you can get first of all, looking for signs of dirt or grease. If they appear greasy but not burned or pitted, push the contacts apart and clean them with a solvent-damped cloth. Then turn the engine over to get the points to their fully-open position as we described in the service information on page 121. Check the gap with the feeler, and reset it if necessary. If the points look in bad condition, replace them according to the instructions on page 120, if you're smart enough to be carrying the spare set we recommended. Alternatively file them to as close to bright metal as you can with a nail-file or, if the worst comes to the worst, with the doubled-over striker off a box of matches. Wipe any dust away with the cloth, reset the points and try again. If the points were the problem, the car should now run.

If the sparking plug test at the very beginning exonerated the ignition, then you have to look elsewhere. The other major area of responsibility for roadside stoppages is:

THE FUEL SYSTEM

Rule One for survival in performing these tests. Don't smoke or allow anybody to bring any naked lights within range.

⋆ **Disconnect the petrol-supply pipe from the carburettor**. You may need a spanner to do this, or have to unscrew a worm-drive clip and pull a flexible pipe off. Remove the **air-filter** housing as well, as we described on page 129, which will make everything much easier to get at. Suspend the free end of the pipe in a clean jar, bottle or tin. Crank the engine over on the starter a few turns, but be careful not to have any disconnected ignition parts sending sparks bouncing all over the place. If there is a **healthy and regular spurting of petrol** from the pipe, this lets the fuel-delivery system off the hook, in other words, the pipes and the pump. Before you leave this, however, examine the fuel you've just collected for signs of water droplets. Water in the fuel is not easily remedied on the spot because you really need to drain the petrol tank thoroughly and blow out the fuel-lines. Assuming this end of the test is OK though, you now look more closely at the **carburettor**.

⋆ **Unscrew the petrol intake on the float chamber**. You may already have had to do this to carry out the first test. If there is a gauze thimble-like filter in the inlet, check for blockages in it and if there are any, wash and blow it clean. If it was severely blocked, it may well have caused your problem. If not:

⋆ **Remove the float-chamber top** and take out the float. Extract the needle valve that bears on it, blow through the parts and carefully clean them with tissue or with a clean and unfluffy rag. The inlet, which is a pretty small aperture, might have been blocked by dirt in the petrol. If you do find a lot of evidence of dirt, the fuel system will need to be cleaned out from tank to carburettor once you're rolling again.

Having cleaned these parts, now:

⋆ **Fill the float chamber** with the petrol you collected at the initial fuel-pump test, replace the top and have someone turn the starter key to crank the engine over while you peer into the carburettor's air intake. If you can see a spray of petrol emerging from the jet in the passageway, your problems may now be over and the car should start. If you can't, it means that one or more of the jets in the carburettor is blocked.

If this is the case, you have slightly more of a problem. If you've already been servicing your car, you'll know where the jets are and whether they're amenable to removal without your having to dismantle the carburettor off the car. If you can readily get get them out, **remove the jets** and blow through them to clear them, but **don't poke them with any metal objects or wire**. Take great care also that in the anguish of trying to cope with all this you don't mix up which jet comes from which hole, or drop any of them into the carburettor air intake, in which event your original difficulties will be as nothing compared with what is to come.

If you *can't* get the jets out easily, then you will have to resort to a tow or a breakdown truck. A last resort is to **remove the mixture-control screw** if your carburettor has an unsealed version of this device, blow into the hole as hard as you can or hold the valve end of your tyre pump against it and pump a couple of times. Then tighten the screw fully in and untighten it again by 1¼ turns to get a starting mixture.

If, on the other hand, there was no petrol at the carburettor inlet when you tried the first test, your supply system has failed — then as long as there's petrol in the tank, you now do the following:

★ **If you have an electric fuel pump**, disconnect the thin wire supplying it with current, wind your test-wire around it and scrape the other end against the earth point with the ignition on, as you did for the ignition tests. If there's *no* spark, then the wiring to the pump is loose or broken somewhere, and you can lash it up to get home by using your test-wire direct from the supply side of the battery to the pump terminal. If there *is* a spark, then:

★ **Take the cover off the pump**. You will see underneath it a pair of contact points very similar to the ones in the distributor. Clean these, but this time simply by pulling a piece of clean paper between them while squeezing them together. Try turning on the ignition again to see if the pump now delivers fuel. If not:

★ **Disconnect the pipe** that brings petrol from the tank to the pump. It's obvious which one this is — it *isn't* the one that runs from the pump to the carburettor. Try blowing hard down this pipe while somebody with good hearing goes to the other end of the car. You shouldn't get apoplectic with the effort and your assistant will hear bubbling in the tank.

If there is a blockage here, further work may be difficult. Fuel tanks are intentionally in out-of-the-way places under the back of the car, and if there's an obstruction in the filter on the pick-up pipe at the tank it may be very hard to reach. Consult your manual. If you can lay hands on a length of petrol hose — accessory shops sell it by the metre — you may be able to rig up a temporary rescue device by connecting one end to the input side of the pump, threading the other through a convenient hole in the bulkhead to the interior of the car and suspending that end in a metal can of fuel.

Once again, **no smoking** if you do this, and drive with the windows open.

★ **If you have a mechanical or cam-driven fuel pump**, remove the top cover by unscrewing the small bolt or screw in the centre. Check that the sealing washer is undamaged — air leaks stop pumps. Check that the pipe unions are tight, and that there are no leaks from any of the pump's gaskets, and blow the gauze filter clean if it looks blocked. Blow through the inlet pipe toward's the tank as in the test we described just now for the electric pump — the get-you-home remedy can be the same. If there's no blockage on the inlet side, no dirt in the filter and the top cover is secure and airtight, then the problem is likely to be a broken spring in the pump, or a ruptured diaphragm. You can't do much about either of these things on the spot.

★ **If faulty pumps are your diagnosis**, whether the system is electrical or mechanical, then at least fitting replacements is only a few minutes' work. This might be a possibility if you're within reach of a service station, a good accessory and spares shop or an agency for your car. Or if you do have to call for help, it will certainly save time all round if you can assure your rescuers on the phone that a new pump is what you need.

OTHER ENGINE BREAKDOWNS

If the car is **overheating**, examine the following:

● **Water-level** — check page 87 on cooling-system designs, and top up if necessary but **don't put cold water into a hot engine.** Wait for it to cool or use hot water.

- **Fan belt** — is it slack or broken? Tighten it if necessary, or replace it with the emergency belt we described on page 85.

- **Thermostat** — check as on page 129.

- **Radiator** — is it visibly leaking? If it's clogged this won't suddenly have caused trouble and you'll have had overheating problems for some time. Remove it and flush it through or have it replaced.

- **Wrong ignition timing** — check the timing as on page 122.

- **Weak fuel mixture** — examine plugs for evidence as on page 126. Check the fuel system for weak pumps, filter blockages, incorrect float-chamber level, blocked jets.

- **Seizing engine** — evidenced as above.

- **Binding brakes** — jack the wheels off the ground and see if there are restrictions to rotation.

- **Water leaks** — examine water-pipe joints, look for burst hosing, leaks around the cylinder-head joint etc. Retighten joints or replace hoses. If there are leaks from the head they may be due to a blown head gasket. No roadside repair is possible and removal of the head and replacement of the gasket is the only remedy.

- **Ice blocking radiator or water pump sheared** — a block of ice might have formed low in the radiator, or the pump may have become damaged in restarting after a freeze-up. This won't have happened if you've attended to antifreeze.

If the car is **overcooling** — in other words if it takes an age to warm up, needs long choke application and the heater is cool, problems may lie in:

- **Faulty thermostat** — once again, check as on page 129.
- **Too large radiator area** — the manufacturers may recommend some blanking off of the radiator surface in very cold weather.

More or less everything else that can happen to your engine will defy roadside repairs. Other faults can include:

- **Blown cylinder-head gasket** — evidenced by oil globules in the radiator or expansion tank, overheating or even visible or audible escapes of gas around the edges of the head. If the car will run, you might limp home, but if it won't, then there are no with-one-bound-they-were-free tips.

- **Seized engine, broken crankshaft or worn bearings, dropped valve** — and other disasters. If the engine is seized, the starter will hardly turn it and it will be almost impossible to push in top gear. Sudden metallic bangs or clattering noises — especially if accompanied by illumination of the oil-pressure light whilst you are driving — should always make you stop while the going's good and get help. A 'dropped valve' means that a valve has come free of its fastenings in the head and hit the top of a piston. At the kinds of speeds engines reach you can imagine what damage that does.

- **Oil-pressure light comes on whilst you are driving normally**. Stop at once. There may simply be an oil leak or a low level of oil in the engine. If you've just let it run low, check the dip-stick and replenish before driving on. If there's a leak, repair it before you go any further. But if the level's normal, suspect serious engine wear. You may be able to hear knocking or clattering from the engine, particularly when taking your foot off the gas to let the car decelerate. The remedy is a replacement engine or an engine rebuild. It is possible to drive the car for a short distance with the bearings knocking, but take it slowly or you may break the crankshaft and inflate the repair bill even further.

We have assumed throughout this book that while you might be willing — and, eventually, able — to perform even quite sophisticated operations on such things as the ignition, the carburation and the cooling systems yourself, substantial dismantling and repair of the car will be something you will pass on to the professionals.

If you *do* want to go further — out of interest, financial desperation, mental instability or whatever — the potential snags should not be underestimated, but neither should they be exaggerated. Remember the obvious — that everything on a car that doesn't require special tools to remove is put together with nuts and bolts. But, unsurprisingly, where undoing two or three nuts to remove the air-cleaner seems manageable to anyone, undoing a couple of dozen to remove the cylinder head, or maybe even the engine itself, seems momentous.

Well, the fact is that it *isn't* momentous, but it takes longer, you have to take more care for more time, and it may be more tiring, require some labouring skills shifting heavy or awkward weights, and be more disheartening if things go wrong. The problem is that as an amateur mechanic you may do such a job very rarely in your life.

Experience as well as good facilities is what lightens the load for the pro. The expert who has done it countless times may have the engine out of the car in an hour. It may take you many depressing times as long if you're ill-equipped, in the open, and pausing end-lessly for consultation, cups of tea and ruminations on what you could otherwise be doing with your life. But if you're going to do it, then patience, attention to detail and scrupulous cleanliness are as critical to the outcome as your tool-kit.

And bear in mind the services that exist to help you. Engine, clutch, gearbox and final-drive specialists all offer guaranteed replacement or exchange units which you can simply drop into place once you have taken out the old one. Some of them also offer dismantling and fitting services at surprisingly cheap rates. If you *do* strip such things down yourself, follow the workshop manual care-fully. Engine reconditioning, if you don't opt for exchange units, is inevitably going to take you to the local motor-machining specialist who can perform such mysterious tasks as crankshaft regrinding, cylinder-head reconditioning and cylinder reboring. Whether the money you will save by doing all the dismantling and reassembly yourself is worth the time it takes you depends on what other calls on your time there are. There *is* a satisfaction in doing it for its own sake. But we have increasingly found as the years pass that the satisfaction is primarily restricted to work on unusual, obsolete or specialized cars and that where there is an existing off-the-shelf service for popular production machines, it makes a lot of sense to use it.

NON-ENGINE PROBLEMS

Clutch. Before doing anything else, check with the manual to find out whether your car's clutch is adjustable, and if it is, get the adjustment right as we described on page 140 if you're experiencing either **clutch slip** (when the engine races but the car doesn't acceler-ate) or **clutch spin** (when you have difficulty in engaging gears). If the adjustment is OK, any other problems over the clutch will involve stripping it down.

Faults in the clutch can include:

★ Oil on clutch plates, faulty release gear, weak springs, worn, distorted or broken plates, centre plate sticking on gearbox shaft, bent shaft, worn release bearing. You will need a service station or a clutch specialist to take the clutch out for examination, unless you feel brave enough to embark on it yourself.

Gearbox. Troubles with gearboxes usually manifest themselves as absence of one or more gears, jamming in one gear or another, jumping out of gear, noise, whine, or lack of output drive. Once again, almost all gearbox problems will mean that it has to be removed and dismantled, but if you experience **stiff action of the selector, difficulty in getting gears, jumping out of gear or engagement of two gears at once**, it may be possible to fix it if the top of the gearbox can be removed without extensive dismantling. If there is a remote linkage from the gearshift to the box, this may have broken or may have become unduly stiff or worn. And if the shift mechanism is OK, remove the gearbox cover if it's accessible, take great care not to lose or drop any balls and springs that may emerge as you do this, consult the manual and check for broken or slipping parts in the selectors, or for weak selector springs. Further work on the gearbox is a job for a specialist.

Transmission. You may encounter trouble here in the form of **knocking or clicking when cornering** on front-wheel drive cars.
This will normally be down to:

★ Worn drive shaft or constant-velocity joints. Follow the workshop manual if you want to chance your arm, or take the car to the service station.

The car may knock or clunk when you abruptly remove your foot from the accelerator, such as when you are travelling downhill in top gear. Problems are:

★ Worn drive-shaft or propeller-shaft couplings, gearbox or final-drive faults. Check for wear in the drive and propshaft joints by gripping the shaft and trying to turn the coupling to see if there's slack in it. If they're all OK, the trouble lies in the gears or their bearings.

General whines, hums and other cacophonies from the transmission are signs of tooth wear, bearing wear and all-round slow decline. Major surgery is the only solution, though use of a thicker transmission oil can sometimes afford a temporary respite.

Brakes. Check also pages 147 to 152 where we dealt with brake servicing. If your braking is simply poor or ineffective, or the pedal needs pumping or feels springy, blame:

⋆ **Maladjusted linings, worn or oil-soaked linings, scored drum or discs, misalignment of shoes, worn rubber parts in the cylinders, air bubbles in the hydraulics.** Service according to our recommendations in the last chapter.

If the car **swerves** to one side on braking, check for:

⋆ **All the above plus loose brake backplate, linings of different types or grades, loose shoe springs.** Service as above.

If the brakes **bind** or stay on, check for:

⋆ **Bad adjustment as above, swollen rubber parts, seized wheel cylinders, kinks in the brake pipes.** Service as above.

Squeaks from the brakes are not uncommon in wet weather, but a constant problem of this kind may indicate **linings of the wrong type, dust or grease in the brakes, or excessive wear**. Strip and check.

If you have a **brake servo** on your car, trouble with it will reveal itself as extra effort you have to make with your foot to get the car to stop. Air leaks in the system are the most likely problem. Refer to the workshop manual for instructions to suit your design.

Suspension. Dealing with suspension trouble nearly always involves serious dismantling, with a good deal of dirt, rusty nuts and cursing thrown in. Repairs are almost certain to drive you to the pro. If you feel crashes and bangs transferred through the roadwheels to your increasingly sensitive posterior, and your car is equipped with **leaf springs** (see page 48), the fault may be:

⋆ **Rusty springs, worn springs that have lost tension, seized shackles (leaf-spring pivots), damaged shock absorbers**. Refer to your manual. If you have the type of leaf springs that can be lubricated, do so. If the car is sagging, or one spring noticeably flatter than the other, the springs will need to be replaced or retempered. If the springs are good, have the shock-absorbers examined by a specialist.

On **coil-spring systems** the problem may also be the shock-absorbers, or:

★ **Seized suspension arms** (see page 103). Professional, please. Very bouncy suspension indicates shock-absorber failure.
Steering and wheels. Remind yourself of our quick checks on the steering on page 103 to 107. **Vague steering and slop at the steering wheel** can indicate:

- **Worn steering swivels, wheel bearings or loose wheel-bearing nuts.** Check for play with wheels jacked up as on page 104.
- **Loose wheels or elongated wheel-nut holes.**
- **Worn ball joints** — check as on page 104.

If the car wanders on the road, check for:

- **Incorrect tyre pressures**.
- **Weight distribution in car uneven**.
- **Worn shock-absorbers**.
- **Seizing or binding in steering** — check with wheels jacked up.
- **Axles loose on springs**.

If the car is suffering from **wheel wobble** check:

- **Wheel balance and steering geometry** — get a specialist with the right measuring gear.
- **Steering gear** — check for worn parts etc. as above.
- **Tyre pressures**.

If you experience unusually heavy or stiff steering, look for:

- **Lack of lubricant** in the steering parts. Refer to manual for requirements.
- **Bent steering parts** — possibly the result of a crash.

Power-steering problems require a visit to a specialist.

Tyres. Any problems with tyres other than incorrect inflation pressure should result in a visit to the tyre specialist. Punctures are repairable if there isn't a tear or split, but don't drive on a punctured tyre or it will quickly become irrepairably damaged. Wear on tyres can also be symptomatic of other running-gear or braking problems, as already outlined on pages 106 and 107.

OTHER ROADSIDE TROUBLES

The procedure for replacing a roadwheel — as long as you possess a decent inflated spare — is described on page 146.

★ **Windscreen breakage** — replace with a temporary screen, or call a windscreen-replacement specialist. In many areas these firms are available at very short notice.

★ **Blown bulbs** — you should carry a spare set of bulbs with you. Removal of the plastic lenses that cover bulb-holders is normally straightforward with a regular or cross-headed screwdriver. Some have to be attacked from inside the car, however. Push and twist the bulbs just like domestic fittings. Sealed-beam headlamps are more complicated to replace and reset.

★ **Exhausts** — if your exhaust falls off or a pipe breaks and starts dragging along the road, you may be able to rig up all manner of lash-ups with wire coat-hangers, pieces of tin cans etc. **Silencer repair kits** are sold in accessory shops and you should follow the instructions on the packet. They will repair splits and holes but will not carry weight or hold together broken pipes, so additional metal reinforcement is necessary for that. Quick-service drive-in exhaust-replacement specialists are increasingly available.

9

BODY LANGUAGE

MY CAR'S BODYWORK AND MY BODYWORK HAVE DEPRECIATED IN THE SAME AREAS, KNOW WHAT I MEAN?

'The bodywork, the lines of union are touched,
the upholstery palpated, the seats tried,
the doors caressed, the cushions fondled
. . . the object here is totally prostituted, appropriated:
originating from the heaven of Metropolis,
the Goddess is in a quarter of an hour mediatised,
actualising through this exorcism
the very essence of petit-bourgeois advancement.'

(Roland Barthes on the Citroen DS, Mythologies)
'S got wheels on it, goes vroom vroom'
(Two-year-old of the authors' acquaintance)

In the course of this book, we haven't gone into much detail about your car's bodywork, despite having emphasized at the beginning that from the opening of the era of monocoque or chassisless motoring, the condition of the tin can is one of the most vital kinds of maintenance of the lot.

The reason for this omission until now is that sheet-metal repair is a specialized trade, and one that depends on specialized — and expensive — equipment. Whether your pride and joy has become structurally damaged or the elements have got a hold in the form of corrosion, there won't be a great deal you can effectively do about it, however willing the spirit. Paint-spraying equipment or welding gear can cost many times what a single effective repair might cost you in a visit to a body-shop, apart from being disheartening to use unless you've had some experience with it before. So with the exception of very minor body repairs to halt depreciation of your car or to make selling it easier, it simply isn't worth it.

We will thus assume for the purposes of this epilogue that either you are contemplating getting the car back into the condition of its best or better days, or you want to get it ready for sale and ensure that it hits its highest price.

Start with simple cleanliness. Begin with the nastiest bits, the underside and the engine compartment. Dealers certainly appreciate the virtues of making the latter look at its best, because it conveys an impression of loving care that extends beyond simply the shine on the coachwork. First take the car to a garage with **steamcleaning equipment**. This treatment will get all the grime, grease and general detritus of the roads off the less accessible parts of the vehicle, and should include cleaning of the engine bay and the power unit itself. If you decide to do this yourself with a degreasing fluid, cover the carburettor and ignition parts with small plastic bags secured against the ingress of water with masking tape, and hose the degreaser off when it's had time to do its work, according to the instructions. If you have any deeply embedded lumps of grime or that malevolent greasy mud that tucks itself away in corners of motor cars, it may be necessary to work it loose with an old blade before you do your final sluicing down.

Now examine the wheel arches, the box sections running from front to back below the doors, the door bottoms and the underside. The car is very likely to be undersealed, but manufacturers' under-sealing — though consumer demand is now forcing it to improve — has not in the past been renowned for its thoroughness, and sub-sequent undersealing after a year or so of use is difficult to be sure of because inaccessible rust may have already got a hold. There are specialists, however, who will offer guarantees on underbody treatment. If existing undersealing has chipped off or been penetrated by stones and subsequently by rust, you should clean down to bare metal and extend this process to an area beyond the immediate dimensions of the damage. Treat with a proprietary rust-killer according to the instructions and then recoat it with a rustproofing compound such as that described below.

The undersides of doors are likely to have drain-holes that enable water to drip out if it has been introduced to the inside of the door via rainy windows or leaky window-channels. Make sure these holes are clear and not blocked by dirt. You may also find in your examination that the car has had a replacement wing or panel that, unlike the rest of the vehicle has not been undersealed. You will have to apply some form of rustproofer to the underside of this if it is not to go the way of all metalwork.

Anti-rust compounds come in the form of paint-like materials that convert the rust into a harmless substance by chemical action and sometimes act as a primer coat at the same time. A variation that can be particularly suitable for underbodies, wheel arches and the insides of doors is a wax-based material that can be applied by pump — with an injector extension for squirting inside doors — or aerosol and therefore involves less grovelling about and disheartening dirt for yourself. It has the added virtue of being able to 'creep' into hidden crevices by electrostatic action, and if used as recommended by its makers it can provide a very effective inoculation against rust.

Once you're satisfied with the out-of-the-way parts, turn to the coachwork. Start by getting the car out of the direct sunlight, and then sluicing it down with a hose to wash the grime and grit away. If it has a vinyl top, use a proprietary vinyl roof-cleaner on this before you go any further. Then use a small quantity of washing-up liquid or a mild car shampoo in a bucketful of water, splash plenty of it over the vehicle, rinse it down and leather it off with a chamois leather. You can, of course, go to the car-wash for this kind of treatment, but in fact handwashing is kinder to the car than using brushes.

If there is no damage on the bodywork that you want to repair, you can then proceed to polishing the car. A good quality wax or polymer polish will hold up for six months or so, so it isn't the kind of treatment you need to give the car every time you wash it. But if it is waxing time, or you want to give the car that extra special gleam before a sale, start by parking it out of the sunlight and then apply the wax to a complete panel at a time using a clean, damp cloth. As soon as you've covered the panel, remove the residue and buff the surface up with a soft, clean cloth. Don't wax a vinyl roof, or any matt black trim you have.

Make a point of squeezing the wax hard against any trim strips and door handles. These areas are major culprits for hidden rusting because rainwater gets behind them and stays there. If you can force a film of wax into the joins, this is much less likely to happen.

If things aren't as amenable to a valeting operation as all that, because your paintwork looks faded and dull, don't despair. There are ways of rescuing it that don't require a respray, though they're hard work — and once done, you'll probably never be able to get away with them again on this particular coachwork. The solution is 'cutting and polishing' — using a mild abrasive liquid or paste to cut a very fine layer of the paint off the faded surface and buff up what remains. Accessory shops will sell such a 'colour restorer', and you should apply it with a soft, damp cloth, rub it in back and forth rather than with a circular movement until the shine appears on each panel (do a panel at a time) and finish it with a soft, dry rag. If it's done evenly, unhurriedly, and with as much attention devoted to the bottoms of doors and wings as to the bonnet, you can be amazed at the result. Once you're satisfied, wax the car after this treatment.

Clean any chrome parts with a proprietary chrome-cleaner. If you want to stop stains returning, an aerosol of tough acrylic varnish will help a lot, but it won't stop rust advancing where it has already penetrated the surface of the brightwork.

Clean the interior of the car with a vacuum cleaner. Replace the pedal rubbers if they're particularly worn, clean the furnishings with a product intended for whatever it is they're made of in your vehicle (vinyl, cloth or, in a luxury car, real leather) and invest in a new set of carpets — they come ready-made and trimmed for most popular vehicles — if yours are beginning to look as if you use the car for agricultural work.

BODY REPAIR

Motor body repair, even in an era in which the original bodies have probably been assembled by robots, continues to be a highly skilled job. It is also one in which possession of the right equipment not only makes things quicker — as it will frequently do with mechanical work — but can make the difference between an imperceptible repair and the kind where your friends have to put their hands in front of their mouths before they can say 'well done'. For some reason, inexperienced body-repairers lose all sense of balance about assessing the quality of their own labours. Applying fresh paint over something may indeed make it look better to the owner than it did before, but remember that the person who doesn't know its every wrinkle as you do will be comparing it with a showroom car, not with yours in a former life. Body repairs and paintwork are *very* hard to perform to 'as new' standard.

Nevertheless, the odd scratches, scrapes and nailhead-sized rust marks can be impressively repaired with care.

Scratches are common, even on relatively new cars. Sometimes, particularly in cities, they are the calling-card of local youth roaming around at a loose end. Occasionally the scratch is so slight that simply rubbing with the abrasive compound we recommend for restoring sheen to the paintwork will restore the original contours. More often, it's deeper, and you will need to secure a 'touch-up' paint — either from the car's agents or from an accessory shop. You'll have to quote the paint serial number (usually marked on an engine-bay plaque that the owner's handbook will tell you the whereabouts of.) A touch-up paint with a small brush included in the cap, is what you're after, so you can run paint directly into the scratch. The technique is worth a few minutes deliberation. Be scrupulously careful not to daub it all over the surrounding paintwork but try to get it exclusively into the blemish, the line of paint really running no wider than the original fault. Once it's dry, you can then give it a *very mild* rub-down with a lot of water and the gentlest of abrasive papers — maybe 600 to 800 grit — to even out the difference in the level between new paint and old. Then polish it up with a very sparing quantity of the rubbing compound as before.

Where there is local rusting on the kind of damage that a fast-moving stone-chipping can cause, get rid of all flaking or lifted paint around it and rub the affected area and its surroundings with 220-grade wet-and-dry paper and plenty of water. 'Feather off' the surrounding paintwork, which means gradually blend the exposed bare metal in to the top coats via gently staggered layers that look a bit like a section through an onion. Preparation is everything in respraying, even the easiest forms of it. Car body paints have very little filling power, so they can't make up for multitudes of former sins. When your rubbing and fettling has left the original rust spot simply as pits and indentations with rust in, kill this with a rust-inhibitor or a combined rust-killer and primer, let it dry, then apply a top coat with the brush and flatten it off and polish as before. If the indentations and pitting are *very* bad then you may need to apply a coat or two of cellulose filler or 'stopper' to bring the surface back to its proper level — when this is dry, rub it down flat with 200- to 400-grade wet-and-dry paper, and finish with the gloss as before.

Much more extensive damage than this, in the form of buckled, creased or dented bodywork, or rust damage that has actually holed the metal, presents far more substantial difficulties. Modern body-restoring materials in the form of plastic resins and fibreglass reinforcing (all of which are available from accessory shops, accompanied by full instructions for their use) appear to make light of them. However, we don't really accept that a fibreglass repair on a big rust hole, for instance, is a lasting solution. Complete replacement of the panel is a much better bet if the car is still a reasonable investment and you want it to hold its value. Filling deep dents with plastic resin is more acceptable, as long as you grind off the paintwork with a power drill and a sanding disc to provide a proper key for the resin and work *very carefully* with successive layers of cellulose putty on top of the resin surface to get as fine, smooth and unwavering a continuation of the surrounding body surfaces as you can before you paint. Use 220-grit wet-and-dry paper for all the intermediate rubbing down, then aerosol-spray a primer that you rub down again with 400-grit wet-and-dry. Finally apply two or three top coats with an aerosol (allowing each one to touch-dry before recoating), gently rub *that* down with 800-grit wet-and-dry, and buff and blend the whole lot into the surrounding paintwork with abrasive rubbing compound. Remember that with some dents — if there hasn't been stretching or creasing of the metal — you can sometimes get behind them and push them back so close to the original contours that only the gentlest of filling jobs will still need to be done on the surface.

You have to be fetishistic about the preparation, or else the repair will never look right, because the mirror-like surface of polished motor paintwork is utterly unforgiving over even the gentlest of undulations. Don't use your eyes to assess the smoothness in the build-up so much as the tips of your fingers, which you should run lightly in all directions over the repair. Run them over the good sections of the panel as well, to get an idea of what you're aiming at.

And when it comes to spraying with aerosols — for either a primer or a top coat — follow the advice the manufacturers provide. Shake them properly or the paint will never match, use abrasive compound on all the surrounding areas of good paintwork to get rid of wax polish and to provide a key, cover with newspaper and masking tape everything you don't want hit by the spray up to a distance of about five inches around the repair, and use the aerosol in short bursts, moving in a steady line along the repair, stopping at the end, returning slightly further down and so on until the job is covered. Don't spray on thick coats — which will run — but do several light ones. And *don't* let the spray mist drift on to rubber seals around the doors, bonnet or boot, or on to chrome strips, trim or lamps. Remember from when we were explaining the ins and outs of examining a potential purchase, how overspray on these areas is one of the giveaways of bad body repairs. If you're covering a chrome strip with masking tape, be as careful as you can to take the tape *right to the edge* of the chrome but not to let it butt on to the paintwork by even a thumbnail's thickness. Run a feeler gauge between the strip and the body if you want to be sure. If you don't do this, the ridge where the newly applied paint ends just before the trim strip will be surprisingly obvious and look awful.

Lastly, clean all your wheels, tyres and any plastic trim — there are special preparations available that do wonders to spruce up all of them — and thoroughly clean windows. To a hardened pro the car may not look as if it has just rolled off the production line, but to most other citizens it may look very close to it. And if your sale doesn't go through, you may even find you've wrought enough of a transformation to want to start the relationship all over again.

INDEX